Praise for *The New Science of Selling and Persuasion*

"Bill Brooks' well-researched book is a powerful tool for every sales force. It should be required reading for sales professionals who seek to develop the way of successful selling in a complex, demanding business arena."

—James Canale, CEO, Net2 Technology Group

"Bill Brooks has the uncanny ability to articulate the truth. I know his message is correct because it resonates with my own heretofore unspoken belief structure. Bill has simply and systematically provided the language that crystallizes thought, the prerequisite to action."

—Mike Pierson, vice president, Beckwith & Kuffel, Inc.

"Bill Brooks has done it again! He has been able to cram decades worth of sound advice into an easy-to-read format. A quick read, but a lifetime of wisdom."

—Colonel Francis M. Mungavin, USAF

"Bill Brooks does it again . . . taking the age-old profession of selling to depths far beyond the motivational platitudes, gimmicky techniques, and multi-step systems. *The New Science of Selling and Persuasion* shows how dynamic companies apply documented principles and build an integrated, accountable, and a sustainable sales culture within their organizations."

—David B. Finch, CEO, ATCOM Business Telecom Solutions

"Coach Brooks' unique combination of insight, innovation, and practical experience delivers yet another superb selling tool that is a 'must read'."

—Allen Fritts, president, Honeywell Fire Systems Group

"Bill Brooks has 'raised the bar' once again with a new and refreshing set of disciplines and ideas on how smart companies and great salespeople sell. *The New Science of Selling and Persuasion* is another of his great common sense, disciplined approaches to selling that will give you a competitive advantage over the competition."

—Gary J. Nutter, vice president of sales and marketing, Gulf South Medical Supply

"In the three years since implementing the ideas expounded by Bill Brooks in his groundbreaking new book, *The New Science of Selling and Persuasion*, we've doubled our revenue on only a 10% increase in new leads."

—John K. Harris, founder and CEO, JK Harris & Company

"Bill Brooks understands that each generation brings with it a new set of values and aptitude. In looking at some of the top companies around the world, Bill has seen the common denominators for success, and has put them to work for companies of all shapes and sizes."

—Ronald C. Johnson, president and CEO, MMD Equipment

"No one has done a better job of keeping up with the emerging sales truths than Bill Brooks. His continuous 'in-the-trenches' research has helped him develop scientific methods for increasing sales that will serve any committed organization well beyond their expectations."

—Michael O'Connor, manager, training and development, Gardner Denver

"Day after day, our organization trudged down the same old sales path, focused only on the next step in the sales process. We never evaluated what was effective and what wasn't. Bill Brooks brought our attention up from the daily sales rut and crystallized a 'new' path focused on the effective keys to a successful selling future. I recommend *The New Science of Selling and Persuasion* for all sales organizations who want a clear, effective path for their future."

—Bob Brobeck, president, Classic Sales and Marketing

"Read it! Live it! Love it! Coach it! Your team and your customers will be astonished!"

—James Barry, CEO, Image Logistics Corp.

"This well-researched book is the ultimate scientific synthesis of art and science. It forges lessons learned from a half century of sales theory and practice into a powerful tool for strategic sales managers—indeed, for the entire sales force!"

—Jonathan R. Craddock, president and CEO, TI WoundCare

"In my opinion, Bill Brooks' epic work separates other works into the realm of nonscience. By raising the bar, *The New Science of Selling and Persuasion* becomes the new paradigm for sales—indeed, for business in general. Essential reading for our times."

—Harvey Shapiro, regional sales executive—Southeast region, CHASE Auto Finance

"Where the science of selling meets the art of persuasion, there you will find Bill Brooks' comprehensive sweep of theory and practice. It is as good a tool as you can find for retooling any sales force to compete in today's turbulent, demanding business environment."

—Lynda McNair, senior vice president, Student Loan Xpress

"This carefully researched book is packed with great ideas on how to create a successful selling organization in today's competitive marketplace. There are great lessons in this book for everyone of us who manages a company."

—John C. Wayne, president, Variform, Inc.

THE NEW SCIENCE
OF SELLING
AND PERSUASION

THE NEW SCIENCE

How Smart Companies and

OF SELLING

Great Salespeople Sell

AND PERSUASION

WILLIAM T. BROOKS

WILEY

JOHN WILEY & SONS, INC.

Published by John Wiley & Sons, Inc., Hoboken, New Jersey.
Published simultaneously in Canada.

For general information on our other products and services please contact our Customer Care Department within the United States at (800) 762-2974, outside the United States at (317) 572-3993 or fax (317) 572-4002.

Wiley also publishes its books in a variety of electronic formats. Some content that appears in print may not be available in electronic books. For more information about Wiley products, visit our web site at www.wiley.com.

Library of Congress Cataloging-in-Publication Data:

Brooks, William T.
   The new science of selling and persuasion : how smart companies and great salespeople sell / Bill Brooks.
      p.   cm.
   ISBN 0-471-46924-6 (CLOTH)
   1. Selling.   2. Sales management.   I. Title.
HF5438.25.B744   2004
658.85—dc22

                                                                    2003022634

Printed in the United States of America.

10   9   8   7   6   5   4   3   2   1

Contents

Preface

Sciences are driven by principles, formulas, and measurable outcomes. Professional selling has the potential to be nearly as predictable and consistent as science if the same rules are applied. However, selling is much more elusive than any pure science. Sales and persuasion is, perhaps, the ultimate human undertaking with as many variables as the people involved can throw at it.

There are, however, any number of underlying principles, predictable patterns, statistical realities, and standards that can be applied across an entire sales organization and with individual salespeople to yield a relatively predictable outcome. Together, these factors form *The New Science of Selling and Persuasion.*

This book is very different from most you've read about sales. It looks across an entire enterprise, while simultaneously taking a look at the individuals who comprise it. It examines what the organization should know about itself while concurrently allowing sales managers and salespeople to take a critical look at both themselves and what the organization provides and, perhaps, doesn't provide both to and for them.

Each chapter contains a *Superior Selling Checklist* and, at the end of the book, there are both organizational and individual audits with 228 essential questions that will allow you to take an in-depth look at exactly what organizations and salespeople should ask themselves about each chapter. Those answers will tell you, in clear terms, exactly how smart a sales organization your company has from the perspective of both the management and salespeople who comprise it. The answers may surprise you.

For over 25 years, we have observed that smart companies share 8 common practices when they sell well. Those 8 practices are thoroughly explained from Chapters 3 to 10. Chapters 1 and 2 deal with the *New Science of Selling and Persuasion* and how to manage it. Chapter 11 contains the 202 Universal Sales Management and Sales Truths of this New Science.

It is my hope that you will find this book as fulfilling to read as it was to write. It is based on over two decades of field work, research, and hard core experience. Far from pure theory, it is, instead, based on observing more than 2,000 organizations from over 500 industries. It is a compilation of observation, interaction, research, and experience with over 500,000 salespeople.

It is my hope that the experience gained through those years has found its way into these pages. I hope that the ideas on these pages find their way into your head, heart, and life.

WILLIAM T. BROOKS

Greensboro, North Carolina

Acknowledgments

Deepest appreciation goes to all of those who have made it possible for me to learn the principles behind doing what I do. My late father, Clifford W. Brooks, was the greatest salesperson I ever knew. My late mother, Angela M. Brooks, was the best cheerleader I ever had. My wonderful wife, Nancy, is the real reason behind any degree of success I've ever enjoyed. Our two sons, Will and Jeb, are outstanding young men that anyone would be proud to call their sons. These five people are the ones who have made the biggest difference in my life. I can only hope that I have made a difference in theirs.

I'd also like to give special thanks to Bonnie Joyce, the anchor of my writing life, whose patience and brilliance has made this book possible. I'd also like to thank Matthew Holt, whose confidence in me to deliver meaningful, valuable work has never wavered.

I'd like to give special thanks to my clients over the years who have actually paid me to learn from them. Hopefully, I have helped them along the way, too.

THE NEW SCIENCE OF SELLING AND PERSUASION

The New Science of
Selling and Persuasion

The twentieth century saw a whole host of changes for sales organizations and salespeople alike. Some changes were good and some were bad. The post–World War II boom spawned a huge influx of dollars, customers, salespeople, and promise. And that boom was especially strong, long, and lasting. The 1950s were a time of marketing innovation, product explosion, and the growth of sales as a profession. It also saw the first significant influx of meaningful sales research, the first broad-based teaching of selling skills, audio recordings outlining sales techniques, motivational rallies, speakers, and sales gurus. It was a veritable free-for-all of capitalistic opportunism and sales education.

The 1960s spawned a whole generation of people who sought their own, unique opportunities for change. Unfortunately, for most of the 1960s generation, aggressive salespeople trained in the 1950s way of selling weren't viewed as kinder, gentler emissaries that change. As a consequence, when the 1960s generation became consumers, they demanded a fresh way of selling that presented a softer approach that was more consistent with their view of the world. The subsequent philosophies and methods of selling were more consultative, less direct, and more customer-focused in orientation than anything that the 1950s sales generation had ever learned or even thought about.

The balance of the century subsequently produced varied and sundry offshoots and mutations of the 1970s versions. For the most part, however, they were all nothing more than derivatives of this original "kinder, gentler" method of selling. And that philosophy continued for another 30 years, well into the end of the twentieth century. Whether it was called consultative, customer-focused, solutions-based, problem-solving needs centered, or whatever title was the brand of the year, they were essentially all the same. And now, into the twenty-first century, there are newer, more complex demands required for superior selling than those approaches could hope to solve. For example, salespeople now need to call on the right level of buyer, cut a wider path and penetrate accounts more deeply than ever before. They need to interact with customers more strategically and to position themselves as business professionals who provide effective, long-term, beneficial solutions. The process has extended far beyond the face-to-face phase of the sale and into all that occurs before and following the sale.

However, even in spite of these new and encompassing demands, there remains a hardcore group of salespeople, sales organizations, and even trainers of selling skills that are throwbacks to the early part of the second half of the last century.

The shocking result is that many of these overly simplistic and misguided practices are still woven into the fabric of some of the world's most sophisticated sales organizations in spite of their best efforts to update and professionalize their salesforces. Unfortunately, a host of these misguided tactics are simple to memorize and recall, roll off of our tongue easily, can lead to quick sales, or are simply so easy to use that they have continued to clutter the landscape of sales even today.

Even though there has been over 50 years of concentrated effort to professionalize sales, the true growth of sales as a profession has stalled because of the stagnating presence of many of these practices. Now, into the twenty-first century, these practices have actually become counterproductive to meaningful selling. In fact, they are so out-of-step with the massive changes that have occurred in the marketplace since the target rich 1990s that they have become the business equal of urban myths . . . outdated, counterproductive practices and beliefs that must be eradicated for the good of salespeople, their profession, and their organizations.

In fact, the massive changes that have occurred over the past few years are so all encompassing and pervasive that to knowingly implement these outdated practices is a sure road to bankruptcy, both personally and organizationally. Smart companies and smart salespeople know that such outmoded practices need to be eradicated quickly. Marketplace changes that have occurred in the past three to five years have clearly mandated it. And mandated it fast.

Let's take a look at six significant changes that have rendered these practices not only worthless but counterproductive:

1. Trust is more essential than ever to the sale.
2. The marketplace has become more crowded, mature, and competitive.
3. Purchasing has become consensus-oriented and based far less on relationships than ever before.
4. The capacity to sell value rather than price has become increasingly more critical in pursuit of organizational sales success.
5. Buyers are looking for advisors and business experts who deliver results that exceed basic expectations. They're not interested in salespeople who are positioned as salespeople.
6. Buying decisions are being made at higher and higher levels due to the strategic ramification of purchases.

There is another group of more sophisticated myths that grew up in the latter part of the twentieth century as well. They were the result of the proliferation of digital technology. These myths sprang from the false logic that through the application of sophisticated digital technology, the fundamental world of sales would be changed forever. And that every sales organization, in order to survive, needed to invest immediately and heavily into that technology. The problem with that logic was that many of the most successful salespeople weren't ready for all of that to happen. The real truth is that technology has proven itself to be a media for generating leads, delivering information, or speeding up transactions—nothing more and nothing less. It was not a whole new way to sell or manage the sales process. It never fully replaced salespeople. And probably never will. It is just faster.

The 21 Biggest Myths of Twentieth-Century Selling

Myth 1: Closing Is the Key to Selling

Fact: Closing sales or finalizing transactions is much more a function of what happens early in the sale than what happens when it is time for a prospect to buy. Great salespeople know that.

Our research clearly indicates that prospects are far more concerned about how a salesperson opens a sale than how he closes it. In fact, prospects are far more concerned about the opening of the process than they are about the actual presentation of the salesperson's product or service itself.

What makes a successful opening? Salespeople correctly practice precall planning, creating the right positioning at the right buying level, building and sustaining trust, asking the right questions, selling value, and handling problems or questions. If salespeople do all of these things properly, prospects will "close themselves" no matter what the size of the sale may be, large or small.

—— *Twenty-First Century Smart Selling Fact* ——
Closing sales is merely a consequence of a series of
correctly orchestrated events that precede it. The key
to a successful sale is how you open it. Not how you
close it. That dictates how and whether you will even
close the sale at all.

Myth 2: People Buy from People They Like

Fact: The real truth is that people buy from those they trust.
For salespeople, being trusted is far more essential than being
liked. We polled several thousand buyers asking them to what
degree they most trusted the salesperson they had bought anything from in the previous 24 months.

The results were startling. Over 60 percent said they
didn't trust them at all. But here's the real shocker. Over 90
percent of that 60 percent said they would never buy from that
person again.[1]

So here's the secret: *Trust supersedes like.* That is particularly true if a salesperson expects to have a long-term sales career based on vertically integrating accounts and working in an
environment that demands relationships versus transactions,
where long-term customer or client retention rather than a deal
a day is essential to career success, where a career as a business
professional is preferred to an amateur who plays at selling.

—— *Twenty-First Century Smart Selling Fact* ——
People buy, long term, from people they trust. Trust
will then transform to like. Not vice versa.

Myth 3: Warm Them Up with Small Talk

Talk to even the most sophisticated salesperson and they will
tell you that they have been taught to "warm their prospects up

---

[1] *Superior Selling Master Guide,* 1998 by North American Sales Research Institute.

with small talk." Our research? Exactly 74 percent of prospects find *unsolicited* small talk to be negative. Another 21 percent claimed that it was neutral (ineffective, but not effective). What does that mean? That it either makes no difference or offends 95 percent of the buyers. This research was conducted with 3,312 buyers of a full range of products and services.[2]

What, then, is a salesperson to do that is the least offensive? It's certainly not what most salespeople have been taught to do for the last 50 years! The safest thing? A simple statement of intention. That only offends 38 percent of the buyers![3]

The universally safest thing to say is something related to helping prospects get what they "want." Unfortunately, most salespeople still believe they are helping people buy what they need. The truth is that people will buy what they need from people who understand what they want. You can bet your last nickel on it. Needs-only selling is just not enough. And it is also twentieth century, not twenty-first century selling.

———— *Twenty-First Century Smart Selling Fact* ————
Prospects don't like unsolicited small talk. If they want to engage in small talk they will. If they don't they won't. It's that simple.

Myth 4: Persistence Is the Key to Sales Success

What good is persistence if a salesperson has no intuitive insight? Again, our proprietary research shows that if a salesperson has the clear and focused intuitive insight to develop a quick perception of whether they're dealing with a qualified buyer, they don't need to be overly persistent. Or, at the very least, they know exactly who to be persistent with in pursuing the sale.

---

[2] *Superior Selling Master Guide,* 1998 by North American Sales Research Institute.
[3] *Superior Selling Master Guide,* 1998 by North American Sales Research Institute.

There is nothing more frustrating for a prospect who has no need, no want, no interest, no desire, no budget, or no inclination to buy a product or service than to be pursued relentlessly by a salesperson who won't take no for an answer.

Our capacity to measure these predispositions has been a major breakthrough for thousands of our clients who now know which of their salespeople are most likely to be correct and intuitive in determining which prospects to pursue and which ones to back away from.

—— *Twenty-First Century Smart Selling Fact* ——
Intuitive insight is far more essential than persistence because being even marginally persistent with a qualified prospect is far more valuable than being aggressively persistent with an unqualified one.

Myth 5: Create a Need and People Will Buy

Twentieth-century salespeople were taught that if they could get in front of enough people, were persuasive enough, and could then convince the prospect that they (1) had a need for the salesperson's product or service and that (2) the salesperson could fill it, sales would flow.

The real truth is that the more a salesperson is in front of people who share the common traits of qualified buyers the more successful that salesperson will be. What are these characteristics? Here they are:

- A perceived or recognized need and a legitimate want for what your product or service represents as a solution they are seeking.
- The level of authority and financial ability to pay for that solution.
- A legitimate sense of urgency to resolve their current situation.

- A strong sense of trust on the part of the prospect toward the salesperson, their organization, and their product or service.
- A clear and open willingness to listen to the salesperson.

You'll note that the first characteristic of a qualified prospect is the "perceived or recognized a need and a legitimate want." Unfortunately, in the competitive marketplace of the twenty-first century, buyers have a multitude of choices and there is such a vast array of options that simply running up and down the street begging for business is a quick way to fail in selling anything.

―――― *Twenty-First Century Smart Selling Fact* ――――
People are far more likely to buy a product, solution, or service if they know they need it than if a salesperson tries to convince them that they should buy it.

Myth 6: Our Product Is Unique

The facts are very clear here, too. No selling organization, company, manufacturer, association, or entity will ever again have a long-standing differential advantage in terms of quality product or service.

Whether that is caused by the elimination of trade barriers, an absence of international pollution laws, digital piracy, corporate espionage, ease of product duplication or relaxed copyright infringements, the result is the same. It will be impossible for any organization to have a corner on any market, anywhere, or for any extended period of time ever again. The world is just too small and technology too available for that to occur.

The result is that sales organizations need to position, bundle, package, and sell their product or service in unique ways. And that is very different from simply selling a unique product. The former is dynamic and evolutionary. The latter is both naïve and foolhardy.

—— *Twenty-First Century Smart Selling Fact* ——
No one's quality, product, or service will remain unique in any marketplace very long.

Myth 7: Experienced Salespeople Don't Need to Prospect

Great salespeople never stop prospecting for business no matter how long they have been selling. Whether it is vertically integrating existing accounts, discovering new applications for existing products with new or current accounts, extensive networking, gaining more breadth or depth in existing accounts, or expanding their network in new, different ways, great salespeople understand something that is very basic.

That twenty-first century selling requires staying on top of every facet of the market. That prospects and customers are downsizing, being bought, sold, or reorganizing constantly. That they need to have extensive depth in every account they have and that when buyers leave, salespeople need to know where they go and with whom they can sustain the old account while pursuing their old customer when they acquire a new position. They also understand that loyalty is not nearly as key a factor as it used to be and that their most loyal, profitable customer is someone else's #1 prospect. They understand that prospecting is the fuel that drives the sales engine whether they have been selling for one year or twenty-one years.

—— *Twenty-First Century Smart Selling Fact* ——
The secret to selling is never only in the act of face-to-face selling. Instead, it is in the constant, consistent art and science of prospecting and positioning. Most salespeople ultimately fail due to a lack of qualified prospects.

Myth 8: Hungry Salespeople Sell Better

This myth goes all the way back to the mid-twentieth century. In those days, you could ask a sales manager to describe the ideal salesperson and they would say, "One with lots of bills." The rationale? They would work hard to get out of debt.

The real truth is that "hungry" salespeople fall prey to the classic, age-old advice that tells us, "A hungry stomach cannot hear." And it is still true that the most essential selling skill of all is the capacity to listen. Smart companies hire and retain salespeople who aren't hungry and inner-focused. Instead, they have salespeople who are totally customer-focused and able to operate from the perspective of satisfying customers rather than satisfying their own desperate need for survival.

——— *Twenty-First Century Smart Selling Fact* ———
Smart companies have salespeople who focus on their customers rather than on themselves.

Myth 9: An Extroverted, Outgoing, Glittering Personality Guarantees Sales Success

This false belief finds itself centered around the cult of personality. That your personality (*how* you sell) is the centerpiece of sales success. It has also been perpetuated by the proliferation of so-called personality tests that are purported to be able to predict who will and who won't sell successfully.

Our research points out in no uncertain terms that salespeople with flexible personalities do, indeed, sell better. However, flexible does not mean "extroverted, outgoing, or glittering." We have also discovered that among thousands of clients, there are factors that are much deeper and more predictive of sales success than the shallow, outward display of your style, known as *personality*. These issues are the successful application of selling skills and product knowledge and the unique combination of values, interests, and personal attributes that yield success on a job-by-job basis. And these measurable and scientifically predictable values, attitudes, attributes, and talents really do supersede the overly simplistic and surface view of "personality."

—— *Twenty-First Century Smart Selling Fact* ——
A flexible personality supported with the right selling
skills and correctly applied product knowledge, coupled
with the right combination of values, attributes, and talents that the job requires guarantee sales success.

Myth 10: Provocative Questions Still Work

If I could show you a way to save money, you'd be interested,
wouldn't you? Whether it is a leading question about saving
money, improving productivity, reducing quality problems, or
gaining greater yield, these questions have been around for
over 60 years. The sad truth? They are still being taught and
used today.

The real truth? They are being met with more and more
resentment by sophisticated twenty-first century prospects.
They have heard them all before. And the more sophisticated
the prospect, the more likely that using them will get a salesperson invited to leave or, at least, never invited back.

What is the prospect supposed to say? "No, I don't want to
save money?" Of course not. And that is precisely the problem.
It is an outdated, old-fashioned ploy. But here is the bigger problem. Words, phrases, and comments like that flow off of people's
tongues with great ease. For example, "If I could show you a way
to get exactly what you need at half the price, you'd be interested, wouldn't you?" That's not selling. It's manipulation.

—— *Twenty-First Century Smart Selling Fact* ——
Provocative questions, although easy to learn and ask,
are manipulative, leading, and deceptive.

People want to see and experience the result you promise,
but don't want to be manipulated into doing so. And, if they
are manipulated, they resent it and will seek future purchases
elsewhere.

Myth 11: Motivation Is the Key to Sales Success

Here is an interesting question to ponder: Does motivation drive performance or does superior performance cause someone to be motivated? It could be argued that everyone is motivated. Some more than others. There are some that are motivated to sell. Others are motivated to be social workers. Others want to be entrepreneurs. Some people want to become managers. Others want to be artists. Clearly, different people are motivated by different things.

Smart companies only employ as salespeople those employees who are motivated to sell within the unique culture of that specific organization. Much more about that later, because, again, all of that is a science that is both measurable and predictable.

The real truth is contained in this simple statement: *There is nothing worse than energizing incompetence.* Great salespeople know how to sell, can sell well, want to sell, can build a productive sales territory, and are then catapulted from that platform into a realm of heightened and sustained motivation based on the successful attainment of the expectations that are held for them. Sound like a mouthful? Here are the facts.

———— *Twenty-First Century Smart Selling Fact* ————
Properly applied product knowledge, selling skills, interpersonal skills, intrapersonal mastery, intelligence, clarity, and focus lead to sales success. That success then creates sustained motivation.

Myth 12: Cold Calling Is a Good Idea

Serious and successful sales organizations that will prosper in the twenty-first century will move past this archaic and self-defeating strategy. Instead, they will understand that there are a whole host of far more productive and powerful ways to prospect for business.

The seriously crowded marketplace of the twenty-first century demands a series of "pull" strategies rather than one, simplistic approach based on "push." For example, aggressive, cold calling totally mispositions a salesperson as a peddler. Networking, authorship, sponsorship, and other more sophisticated strategies position salespeople as advocates, business experts, industry supporters, or niched industry gurus to whom interested prospects turn for solutions and sources. There is little doubt that running up and down the street or banging the telephone hoping to find someone who will listen to your message falls far short of having salespeople invest valuable face-to-face selling time with people who are eager to see them and are truly qualified prospects. These are the ones who have all of the five qualities we have identified as being necessary in defining a truly qualified buyer.

────── Twenty-First Century Smart Selling Fact ──────
A full battery of pull-prospecting strategies is necessary to ensure that salespeople are investing valuable face-to-face selling time with the right people. Of all the options available, cold calling is, by far, the least effective for accomplishing this.

Myth 13: Great Salespeople Make Superior Sales Managers

This gigantic myth will be explored in much greater detail later. However, at this point, it is sufficient simply to dismiss this logic as being flawed from the beginning.

Sales and sales management require different skills, behaviors, talents, and competencies. It is not unusual to see a top-performing salesperson fail miserably when moved into a sales management position. There are many reasons for this that will be discussed more thoroughly later.

A strong argument could be made that sales managers must have a totally different way of thinking from that required of salespeople. Their job is far more strategic and often more systematic. Sales management positions require a great deal more coordination between constituencies; a certain amount of political know-how; and the patience to deal with issues, policies, bureaucracy, and internal politics. Those positions also demand interaction with a multitude of internal constituencies coupled with the capacity to engineer sophisticated, multifaceted outcomes that most sales positions rarely require.

The real facts are these: Highly productive salespeople become successful because of their abilities to do far different things. What, therefore, makes an organization automatically believe that the same person should be able to (or even want to) completely change identities and meet a totally different set of job demands?

———— *Twenty-First Century Smart Selling Fact* ————
Great salespeople often make mediocre or poor sales managers. The skills and mind-set required for success as a sales manager are far different and require a very different set of capacities than sales.

Myth 14: Prior Industry Experience Is a Guarantor of Sales Success

This myth leads to the corporate bondage scenario. We have had untold clients over the years who have insisted that they only hire salespeople who have had extensive industry experience. When replacing salespeople they were, therefore, limited to the ever-shrinking pool of top talent that came only from within their industry.

The result? Employing retreads, hiring a competitor's disgruntled employee, discovering that the people they thought were great performers really had little talent but had been selling in a target-rich environment, hiring people who had strong product knowledge but no sales skills, and disappointment after disappointment.

Prior industry experience can actually be a detriment when it comes to learning a competitive line, learning about new applications, giving up old loyalties, or even having the energy to start something all over again. By the same token, if you believe that the salespeople will bring business with them, think again. Customers have, ultimately, been buying from the organization, not from the salesperson unless churning customers is common in the industry in which they sell. Switching their customer to a new product or employer may require nothing more complex or sophisticated than a simple signature change.

—— *Twenty-First Century Smart Selling Fact* ——
Previous industry experience could mean leaving failed relationships, inadequate training, and running from one job, or bad situation, to another. Be cautious. Be sure you don't hire your competitor's problem.

Myth 15: New Products Will Automatically Improve Sales

You need to look no further than your ratio of successful versus failed new products to see the fallacy in this belief. Sometimes even great products hitting the market at the right time with the right solutions can fail with little of the failure landing at the feet of the product itself.

Smart organizations understand precisely why they are releasing new products or introducing new services. They also know the exact way to train salespeople to understand, develop belief in, and sell new product releases. As many new products fail because of inadequate preparation and training of the salespeople to sell them as fail because of being a flawed product.

—— *Twenty-First Century Smart Selling Fact* ——
Better professional selling will improve the chance of success for any new product. It takes even great salespeople time to learn how to sell *any* new product or service.

Myth 16: Sales Automation Will Solve All of Our Problems

According to *BusinessWeek* (June 23, 2003), the problem behind this myth is simple. Their headline? "It's too complicated. It's too expensive . . ." They were talking about business software in general. However, our experience could echo the same sentiment as related to a vast percentage of enterprise-wide salesforce automation initiatives.

For most salespeople, simple is better. Particularly when it comes to digital tools. The problem? Salespeople don't usually purchase the software. Someone else somewhere in the organization makes the purchase decision and then salespeople are told to use it. According to the same article, "analysts estimate business-software customers spend $5.00 installing and fixing their software for every $1.00 they spend on software." And this ratio could be worse when you look at the sales arena where you must factor in lost sales time, decreased morale, and the confusion that salespeople have when they are attempting to make the latest software initiative work while they are simultaneously trying to prospect, sell, and service accounts.

—— *Twenty-First Century Smart Selling Fact* ——
Salespeople should spend their time at what they do best: Selling. Becoming a data entry clerk simply for the sake of data gathering is not the primary job of a sales professional.

Myth 17: Most Salespeople Fail because They Can't Handle Rejection

We have assessed literally tens of thousands of salespeople over the past two decades in very sophisticated ways. That experience has shown us that well over 85 percent of the salespeople we have evaluated have no problem whatsoever with rejection. In fact, the data shows that for the vast majority of salespeople it is not even an issue.

The real issues are generally a lack of self-starting ability, lack of enjoyment of the sales role, poor commitment to the job, fear of embarrassment, or poor goal direction. Whether veiled as call reluctance or the classic inability to handle rejection, this overly simplistic view is a clear case of mislabeling the cause of something that leads to specific outcome. The outcome? Salespeople making too few calls.

We need straightforward answers to complex problems. However, to get to those usable answers, it is necessary to have the right data relative to what drives the outcome in the first place. And, sometimes, these are complicated factors that are not as simplistic as we would like them to be.

―――― *Twenty-First Century Smart Selling Fact* ――――
Rejection is not a problem for most salespeople. Instead, a combination of other factors lead to salespeople making too few calls.

Myth 18: Sales Is a Volume Game

Let there be little doubt about it. Any organization could easily go bankrupt selling nothing but volume. In fact, you could be selling so much that you don't even know how much money you are losing. Successful selling is more often a function of margin than it is of volume.

The most effective sales organizations are the ones that have most of their salespeople consistently selling high volume at high margin. In fact, we have literally hundreds of clients with whom we have worked to convince that this should be their major, single sales goal.

Here's how it works. Salespeople can give products or services away simply to make a sale. There are others who will stick by their guns in terms of margin, but, unfortunately, won't necessarily sell products or services at a volume that even substantiates their continued employment. However, there are those select few who, with the right set of tools, skills, support, and coaching, can sell high volume at high margin and tend to do so on a consistent and regular basis. The smart selling company will do all in its power to populate its salesforce with those who can sell that way.

───── *Twenty-First Century Smart Selling Fact* ─────
In the final analysis, sales is all about margin. Great salespeople, however, sell high volume at that high margin. And they do it with great consistency.

Myth 19: Good Salespeople Can Sell Anything

Wrong! There is a significant difference between selling different types of things. Products versus services. Tangible versus intangible. Big ticket versus smaller ticket. Business-to-business versus business-to-consumer. Demand versus nondemand. Complex versus simple. Senior level selling versus staff level selling. Frequent versus infrequent. Technical versus nontechnical. Put the combinations together and it is mind boggling.

This, however, creates a problem that we have discussed and will discuss again elsewhere. The same old problem comes up again and again. Employers tend to gravitate toward hiring only salespeople who have had previous industry experience. However, this does not have to be the case. The solution is fairly simple.

Salespeople tend to do well if they stay within a general category. For example, if someone has had experience selling a nondemand, high-ticket, complex product to senior-level executives, there is great carryover from selling in one environment like that to another. However, to hire someone who has had previous experience selling purely demand, smaller ticket, simple offerings to lower level buyers for that job would not make much sense.

And remember, it doesn't have to be industry specific. But it should be category specific. For example, if an organization needs to hire someone to sell earth-moving equipment, it would not be too radical a departure to hire someone with a background in selling other types of industrial equipment (trucks, compressors, batteries, high-end pumps, etc.). But to go into that sales situation directly from the retail selling of lower priced products where customers come to you and buy spontaneously is a sales disaster waiting to happen.

―――― *Twenty-First Century Smart Selling Fact* ――――
The critical question to ponder is how well a salesperson will perform in your unique, one-of-a-kind job environment and within the cultural demands of your organization.

Myth 20: Motivation Is the Key to Sales Success

VICE PRESIDENT OF SALES: Can you come in next month and fire up our sales team at our annual sales meeting?

ME: How well have they been performing?

VICE PRESIDENT OF SALES: Not good. That's why we need a motivational speaker.

ME: Have you thought about supplying them with better insight and skills and then determine what is causing them problems?

VICE PRESIDENT OF SALES: Why?

This short, but real-world dialogue makes the whole point. But first, let me ask you a question similar to the one asked earlier in this chapter: Does motivation drive successful sales performance or does experiencing sales success spur a higher level of motivation?

On one hand, a person needs to be motivated to perform. On the other, success does breed success. Here's the answer: All people are motivated by something. Unfortunately, not all are motivated by the things that drive superior sales performance. Some people are in jobs that don't reward the things that they want to be rewarded for, that is, delivering superior performance. And the real truth is that short-term, hype-'em-up speeches just don't work. In fact, as a college football coach for 14 years, I can tell you that pregame or half-time speeches don't have much of an effect. Belief in the game plan and coaches, a series of back-to-back wins, a successful 14-play drive—these are the things that contribute to sustained motivation.

—— *Twenty-First Century Smart Selling Fact* ——
Motivation is only a portion of the sales success formula. Properly applied product knowledge, selling skills, strong interpersonal skills, and enjoying the success sales can bring are just as important and lead to sustained motivation.

Myth 21: Good Salespeople Get More Objections

Objections are nothing more than a sign that a salesperson is showing the wrong thing in the wrong way. What it means is that the prospect is simply saying, "Stop, I've heard enough!" Wouldn't it make more sense to determine precisely what the prospect wants, the conditions under which they will pay to get it, the time frame in which they will buy it, how much they are willing to pay for it, and the process by which they will buy it *before* making a presentation? Then show your product in precisely that way.

The real truth is that great sellers deal with far fewer objections than average or poor ones do. The reasons for that are that they are confident, have positioned themselves well, do intensive precall planning, develop strong internal advocacy, build trust, ask the right questions, propose the right solutions, solicit feedback, and create value. The result? Very few, if any, objections ever arise.

A misguided corollary to this myth is the mistaken belief that objections are a sign of interest. The failed theory behind this myth is that the salesperson is moving closer to the sale and that through a series of rehearsed maneuvers will be able to handle each objection, squash each one verbally, and then move on to make the sale.

The truth is that in the twenty-first century, poorer salespeople get most of the objections. The reason is that the great salespeople painstakingly uncover each issue through careful research, accurate questioning, and a finely honed presentation that addresses each prospect's unique concerns. As a result, fewer objections ever arise. The poor ones? They do none of that. They just deliver one canned presentation after another.

—— *Twenty-First Century Smart Selling Fact* ——
Great salespeople get fewer objections because they develop serious prospect interest in their product or service through a perfectly crafted presentation based on research, trust, and meaningful questioning.

Some of these myths will be revisited in upcoming chapters. However, it was essential to present them as a precursor to everything that this book is all about. Why?

Because the twenty-first century has demanded a new science of selling and persuasion. This is a time characterized by a broad array of complex demands that will grow more intense daily for salespeople and their organizations. Intensified competition, reverse Internet auctions, spreadsheet buying, and price-driven decisions are just the beginning.

As we move forward, it will be essential that great salespeople, enlightened sales management, and smart companies unshackle themselves from the myths of the past. To continue going forward with these same outdated and inaccurate strategies will be tantamount to performing sales suicide. And great salespeople and smart companies don't want to do that.

CHAPTER 1
THE SUPERIOR SELLING CHAPTER REVIEW

- The twentieth century launched sales as a profession.
- There were significant changes that occurred in the latter half of the century.
- A softer, gentler approach to sales blossomed after the 1960s.
- Most selling philosophies in the latter half of the century centered around consultative selling.
- Many old-school selling techniques are for the most part, manipulative and deceiving.
- Some of these old-school techniques are, unfortunately, still in use today.
- They have led to some myths that have continued today.
- These myths have been replaced by smart selling facts. These myths and facts are:

  Myth 1: Closing is the key to selling.

  Fact 1: Closing sales is merely a consequence of a series of correctly orchestrated events that precede it.

  Myth 2: People buy from people they like.

  Fact 2: People buy, long term, from people they trust.

  Myth 3: Warm them up with small talk.

  Fact 3: Prospects don't like unsolicited small talk.

  Myth 4: Persistence is the key to sales success.

  Fact 4: Intuitive insight is far more essential than persistence because being even marginally persistent with a qualified prospect is far more valuable than being aggressively persistent with an unqualified one.

  Myth 5: Create a need and people will buy.

  Fact 5: People are far more likely to buy a product or service if they know they need it than if a salesperson tries to convince them that they should buy it.

Myth 6: *Our product is unique.*

Fact 6: No product will remain unique in any marketplace very long.

Myth 7: *Experienced salespeople don't need to prospect.*

Fact 7: The secret to selling is not in face-to-face selling.

Myth 8: *Hungry salespeople sell better.*

Fact 8: Smart companies have salespeople who focus on customers' needs and concerns rather than on their own.

Myth 9: *An extroverted, outgoing, glittering personality guarantees sales success.*

Fact 9: A flexible personality supported with the right selling skills, applied product knowledge, values, attributes, and talents that the job requires guarantee sales success.

Myth 10: *Provocative questions still work.*

Fact 10: Provocative questions, although easy to learn and ask, are manipulative, leading, and deceptive.

Myth 11: *Motivation is the key to sales success.*

Fact 11: Properly applied product knowledge, selling skills, interpersonal aptitude, intrapersonal understanding, intelligence, and focus lead to sales success.

Myth 12: *Cold calling is a good idea.*

Fact 12: A full battery of pull-oriented prospecting strategies is necessary to ensure that salespeople are investing valuable face-to-face selling time with the right prospects.

Myth 13: *Great salespeople make superior sales managers.*

Fact 13: Great salespeople often make mediocre or poor sales managers.

Myth 14: *Prior industry experience is a guarantor of sales success.*

Fact 14: Previous industry experience could mean poorly defined relationships, inadequate training, and running from one job, or bad situation, to another. Be careful.

Myth 15: *New products will automatically improve sales.*

Fact 15: Learning how to sell a new product will improve the chance of success for any new product.

Myth 16: Sales automation will solve all of our problems.

Fact 16: Salespeople should spend their time at what they do best.

Myth 17: Most salespeople fail because they can't handle rejection.

Fact 17: Rejection is not a problem for most salespeople.

Myth 18: Sales is a volume game.

Fact 18: In the final analysis, sales is all about margin. Great salespeople sell high volume and high margin and they do it consistently.

Myth 19: Good salespeople can sell anything.

Fact 19: The critical question to ponder is how well will a salesperson perform in your unique, one-of-a-kind job environment and within the cultural demands of your organization.

Myth 20: Motivation is the key to sales success.

Fact 20: Motivation is only a portion of the sales success formula. The truth is that success fuels motivation.

Myth 21: Good salespeople get more objections.

Fact 21: Great salespeople get no objections because they developerious prospect interest in their product or service through a perfectly designed presentation based on research, trust, and meaningful questioning.

The twenty-first century is more competitive, demanding, and less forgiving. A new, more scientific approach is needed. This book will tell you, your organization, and salespeople how to implement that new approach.

Sales Management

Over the course of the past two decades, I have had the rare privilege to personally coach, lead, train, address, or interact with more than 100,000 sales executives or managers and more than 500,000 salespeople. This involvement has been with organizations from over 500 varied industries and with thousands of different organizations worldwide.

I have enjoyed extensive, intensive, in-depth involvement with these people and their organizations. Over this time, I have identified a set of universal sales management and sales truths that transcend whatever product or service is being sold, the customer base it is being sold to, price points, sales geography, or market demands. These truths have been tested, proven, and honed in the field and not in the lecture hall or classroom. They are based on millions of air miles, thousands of automobile travel miles, and interfacing with tens of thousands of salespeople and sales executives.

In any venture, certain underlying principles need to serve as the foundation for any ongoing strategy. Whether these principles relate to medicine, war, or sales management, there are guiding principles or benchmarks that help practitioners of any discipline stay on target and consistently get traction as they move ahead in their chosen field.

The 12 Most Fundamental Sales Management Truths

This chapter outlines the 12 most fundamental sales management truths observed in the most successful sales executives and sales managers I have worked with over the years. Each of these principles serves as a philosophical pillar to help build the infrastructure behind the eight common practices that smart selling companies share when it comes to organizing and leading a successful sales organization.

But before we list and discuss the truths, we need to take a hard and critical look at the realities behind how people tend to become sales managers or executives in the first place. In a recent survey that we conducted, more than 68 percent of the organizations polled indicated that they promote people to sales management positions solely from within their salesforce, and a whopping 85 percent indicated that successful prior sales success was either extremely or somewhat important in that selection. On the other hand, a surprisingly 40 percent indicated that they do not provide any formal sales management training for these new appointees. Of those who do provide training, 55 percent indicated that it was some form of internally developed program.

It is probably safe to conclude that the following conditions apply:

- Many organizations promote people to sales management positions from within.
- They assume that successful selling automatically translates into being a successful sales manager.
- A large number provide no training to be a sales manager.

- Most of those that do train sales managers rely on their own, homemade programs.

You can draw your own conclusions about the efficacy of these conclusions. However, there are some holes in each of these actions—just as there are equally as many valid points that are implicit in decisions that organizations make. It is important to note that:

- Selling and managing are two very different positions with different demands and expectations.
- People need to be trained or educated about those demands and expectations along with exactly how to fulfill them.
- Best practices are, most often, a combination of those that are brought in from the outside and those that are developed internally.

The world of business is often deluged with either high-drift philosophies or with a scattered series of loosely constructed how-to's that are, somehow, supposed to be tied to some sort of ongoing strategy. Unfortunately, many of the how-to-do-it tricks of the trade have been handed down from one generation of sales managers to another. Times have changed, however, bringing a set of much higher expectations for sales managers. And the old things just don't work anymore.

The result has been a disjointed series of maneuvers, tricks, or tactics that lead people nowhere. And, worse yet, with the complex demands of mature markets, more discriminating customers, reduced loyalty, the diminishing importance of relationships (there is even an attempt by some buying organizations to systemically eliminate relationships from the sales process), and a host of new and confusing signals, there is a need to completely reengineer the processes of sales management and sales.

I recently worked on an assignment with a client that sells industrial products. Together, we saw a competitor lose a sale by less than $10 on a $5,500 product. Their customer, one of the world's best-known and recognizable organizations, had posted an auction on the Internet soliciting bids. This, unfortunately, appears to be something that will increase in the future. The organization with whom I was working elected not to bid on such a basis. However, their competition did and waited until the 11th hour, bid less than $10 lower than another competitor, and got the sale. This occurred on the heels of a conference to which our client was invited where all vendors were told: "Take the word *relationship* out of your vocabulary." They were told that everything would be very different going forward. And it was. For example, that same organization has now advanced its auction process to be a reverse auction, allowing other bidders to extend the deadline on the lowest price so they can match or beat it. Who wins there? I believe you know. And it's not the seller. One side always loses in this scenario.

What does this mean to you and your organization? Simply that the world of sales will never be the same again. The landscape has changed forever. Consequently, all of us need a set of solid, proven principles that can guide us going forward. These principles need to be consistent for both sales management and salespeople, and they must be easily and consistently applied both by and across the entire enterprise.

There is little doubt that salespeople never perform any better than their environment allows them to perform. There should also be little doubt that sales managers who are not given adequate responsibility coupled with the appropriate level of authority will only be frustrated—right along with the salespeople who report to them. But much more about that later.

Given these realities, let's look at the 12 *universal sales management truths*. These truths will prove to be effective for *any* sales organization anywhere because they are exactly what we are calling them—*universal* truths:

1. A sales organization will never be any stronger than the salespeople who are recruited, selected, and hired to be a part of it.

2. Invest your time where it counts: with the best performing salespeople and with those who hold the greatest potential for superior performance.

3. A sales organization cannot be led from behind a desk.

4. The best sales executives and sales managers are the most skilled at judging talent and placing the right people in the right place.

5. You can't lead where you won't go any more than you are able to teach the things you don't know.

6. Salespeople must be hired with caution, launched with clarity, and the underperforming ones replaced with dispatch.

7. Pay plans are essential to sales performance and should, ultimately, determine how much of what gets sold.

8. Turnover in a salesforce is normal and to be expected. Zero turnover is bad, but too high a turnover is even worse.

9. Sales executives must never allow digital solutions to dominate a salesforce's life, stifle creativity, or curtail proactivity.

10. You cannot motivate salespeople; you can only create an environment that rewards the things they are most motivated by in the first place.

11. No salesperson will ever reach any meaningful level of performance if expectations are not clearly established, communicated, and verified for their acceptance and total understanding.

12. Performance counts in sales but it is accountability that really pays.

Chapter 12 of this book provides 90 more of these truths that you can apply at various times and in varying circumstances. However, these 12 are the most fundamental and form the basis for the entire system of the new science of selling and persuasion.

Let's take an in-depth view of each of the 12 in greater detail. Please remember, however, that each of these rules has a clear genesis that lies in effective selection, meaningful orientation, and an ongoing training process. These 12 also point out the need to have an environment that allows for creativity coupled with meaningful, in-the-field involvement of sales managers to course-correct, establish accountability, and reward positive performance. That's what smart companies and effective sales management teams do. And they do it all well.

Truth 1: A Sales Organization Will Never Be Any Stronger Than the Salespeople Who Are Recruited, Selected, and Hired to Be a Part of It

A great parallel here is the recruiting strategy employed by the U.S. Army. After the Vietnam War, it was clear to military leaders that drastic changes needed to be made. That unpopular war had led to the massive drafting of unwilling conscripts. Drug use was rampant, the educational level of soldiers was at a very alarming low, overall morale was poor, and performance was spotty at best because of all of these converging factors.

The military decided to do a complete makeover. Efforts to build an all-volunteer Army were initiated. The qualifying standards were beefed up, and a new and more rigorous regimen was introduced. The results were (and are) startling and magnificent.

What does this have to do with your sales organization? Probably more than you think. How selective are you? How thoroughly do you screen applicants? How rock solid is your recruiting process? Is your organization an attractive place to be? What are your standards? Are you constantly raising the bar for entry? Are you always recruiting—even when you don't need salespeople?

The first step in any organization's successful sales journey is to insist on having *only* great salespeople. It's as fundamental as that. We discuss this process in greater depth in Chapter 3.

As previously mentioned, I spent 14 seasons as a college football coach. The parallel among the Army, a salesforce, and the football teams I coached is very clear. When I recruited great players, we won. When I didn't, we lost. It's that simple. That's why this truth forms the bedrock and is the benchmark for all that follows.

Truth 2: Invest Your Time Where It Counts: With the Best Performing Salespeople and with Those Who Hold the Greatest Potential for Superior Performance

Here's the challenge. No matter what your position in life may be, whether it's a CEO, vice president of sales, regional sales manager, president of a country, or the general of an army, there is one common characteristic: Each has an equal allotment of time. We all have 168 hours a week, 52 weeks a year. You can't buy more, barter for more, lease more, or even manufacture more. The most fundamental sales management success factor centers on this simple reality. And your success will ultimately be defined by your answer to this question: How well do you maximize the time you have?

It's not unusual for sales executives or managers to spend (or waste) most of their time on issues created by salespeople whose potential is limited or whose performance is subpar, for example:

- Calming upset customers, prospects, or coworkers.
- Correcting errors and mistakes.
- Coaching and redirecting.
- Providing emotional support.
- Traveling to assist in failed sales efforts.
- Answering redundant questions.
- Seeing no return on the investment made into subpar performers.

- Endlessly wondering why performance fails to get better despite all your work.

Here's the bottom line. You need to ask yourself two very important questions. Would you get a better return on your time if you invested more of it with top performers who, with a slight modification to their current practices, could become great performers? Or, are you better off being dragged into issue after issue and problem after problem that the subpar performers seem to create? The answer should be obvious.

Most people fundamentally know what they should do. They just can't or won't do it. I recall working with a large, well-known nationwide sales organization years ago. It was large enough to prove that the familiar 80/20 rule is still alive and well. A minority of their top performers delivered the majority of the sales. The vast number of their salespeople in the middle (60 percent) delivered steady and consistent performance. The problem was that the bottom 20 percent was demanding as much as 80 percent of their sales management team's time. They were busy working in the bottom rather than on the top. We made a conscious decision that the sales management team should invest 80 percent of their time with the top performers—the salespeople who were deemed to hold the most promise for the future.

The results were startling. The sales management staff became invigorated instantly. They were now working with positive, upbeat, and receptive people who appreciated their time and expertise. Good salespeople became great. Average ones got better. Sales improved.

What about the poor performers? Some got better fast. They solved their own problems, sought their own answers, and lost their enablers—the sales management team. They learned to stand on their own two feet and perform for the first time.

What about those who failed to perform? They probably shouldn't have been there in the first place. They were replaced with people whose standard for selection was higher, more rigorous, and demanding.

This process required the creation of a set of straightforward and enhanced performance standards as well as higher expectations from the poor performers. Smart companies simply don't allow unhappy salespeople or poor performers to hang around very long. A process for solving performance problems and then moving on has to be established and implemented. Sound harsh? In today's marketplace, if you have too many subpar performers, your entire organization may not be around very long. So move fast. Make your decision. Play with the first team. Championship teams can't win with the second team. It's just that simple.

Truth 3: A Sales Organization Cannot Be Led from Behind a Desk

We recently worked with a national sales organization. The newly appointed vice president of sales engaged our firm to help him assess his sales team and make recommendations going forward. We had worked with this same executive on two previous occasions with other sales teams, so we knew his methods and standards. He had participated in our sales management clinics and symposiums on several other occasions, so he knew our methods and standards.

In his usual manner, he took six months to get his own reading before calling us in to help. The organization's market share had dropped, sales volume had plummeted, profits had disappeared, morale had dissipated, and the future had gotten progressively bleaker as each month passed. He had been brought in to fix the problem. We were to be part of his solution.

I dispatched one of our consultants to travel with several salespeople, spent time interviewing sales managers, and did our usual due diligence. Our client had remained relatively quiet, wanting us to reach our own conclusions by making our own observations. We quickly saw what we knew he had begun observing for several months.

The day came for our meeting. We entered the room and our client asked with a wry smile on his face, "Well, what did you find out?" My answer was twofold: "I'll give you the good news first, then the bad news."

The good news? His sales team was enthusiastic, although a bit nervous. They were hungry to get better. They knew they needed help. The bad news? Not one salesperson had seen a sales manager in the field for more than three years.

Our client stood up and said, "Truth 3. You can't lead a sales organization from behind a desk. That has got to stop now."

No one ever gets any better at anything unless he or she is observed, coached, course-corrected, and managed in the field. A good friend of mine puts it this way: "If a picture is worth a thousand words, an experience is worth a thousand pictures."

Any information a sales manager receives without going into the field is pure secondhand information. It is not experiential evidence. It is impossible to get a sense of how effective or ineffective a salesperson is without firsthand, on-the-scene, real-time observation. And real, valuable, first-hand knowledge cannot be gleaned from sales reports, database results, product inventory reports, call sheets, or even sales results. You need to be at the point of attack to determine the effectiveness of your team's effort.

However, it is much easier to stay in the office. It's not nearly as dirty or dangerous. It's not as physically demanding, either. In fact, it can become downright habit forming. The downside is that your sales team can also develop habits without being observed and course-corrected. Unfortunately, those habits are usually bad ones that are difficult to change. Unlearning something is much more difficult than learning something.

Truth 4: The Best Sales Executives and Sales Managers Are the Most Skilled at Judging Talent and Placing the Right People in the Right Place

The ability to judge talent is essential. Placing that talent in the right place is the other half of the formula. I had five uncles, all of whom were thoroughbred horse trainers. My grandfather had done the same thing in Ireland, so his five sons followed his career path here in the United States. I can recall hearing my uncles using the phrase repeatedly, "There are courses for horses." Here's what they meant. Some horses were better at greater distances; others, at shorter ones. Some were better on dirt than on grass. Some were better if they broke from certain starting positions. I remember my uncles withdrawing horses from races if they had a starting position that was not right for the horse.

But the real secret to their success lay in their uncanny ability to identify a good horse when they first saw it. I remember one of my uncles saying, "It doesn't make any difference what course the horse is on if she just can't run. The real gift is to be able to identify good horse flesh in the first place."

At the risk of oversimplifying, the same is true for salespeople. You must first become good at identifying talent. But this is not as easy as it might first appear to be. What is it that makes a salesperson a real champion? Is it intelligence? skill? attitude? sales aptitude? personality? values? product knowledge? industry experience? drive? interpersonal skill? image? It is all of these plus more.

The bottom line is that you cannot determine someone's potential through any form of superficial, hasty evaluation. Instead, this process needs to be well conceived, finely developed, in-depth, and carefully orchestrated. In some cases, it might involve a team of people, but in every case it needs to be extensive enough to look at every essential factor and to include a person's performance over time, psychological components, skills, attitude, manners, character, experience related to previous sales results in your category of sales, and much more. Then it's all about their fit to the job and how well they are managed and coached.

The placement of sales talent is critical. Some people are comfortable with acquiring new business; others are happier serving existing accounts. Some are gifted at complex sales;

others, with transactional ones. Others can easily sell tangible, demand products while some are gifted at selling nondemand, intangible ones. Some can sell big-ticket items. Some can't. Others can make one or two sales a year while some need the thrill of daily or weekly sales. There are others who love selling new products . . . while others can sell only proven, tested ones.

I once worked with a client that had a salesperson who had come to them with outstanding credentials. He appeared to have it all. All of his assessment scores were outstanding. He had been an award-winning salesperson for a very large tangible goods manufacturer. The product he sold was a high-demand one that was so good it was sometimes sold on an allocation basis. It all looked good. But something went wrong. Very wrong.

After a year, he was struggling. In fact, he was far more than suffering. He was in agony. Each month he was at the bottom of the sales ladder. His problems included:

- He had gone from a highly structured corporate environment to one that was entrepreneurial and far more direct sales oriented and less systems driven. The pace was faster, more rigorous, and demanded daily results and high levels of consistent proactivity. Every day demanded a Super Bowl performance and maximum effort.
- He was selling a nondemand, intangible set of products and services rather than the high-demand, tangible ones he had sold before.
- He did not have a set group of customers whom he had inherited in a territory as his book of business. Instead, he had to create new accounts virtually daily.
- He had to sell more creatively and strategically. His previously successful sales experience was based on heavy marketing that created a demand based on seasonality and filling retail inventory.

Unfortunately, these were a set of problems that were virtually insurmountable for this salesperson in his new environment. Sadly, he never did overcome the challenges.

Here's the real issue: How well will a salesperson sell in your unique environment? This is far more than asking if that person has had relevant or related industry experience. Instead, it deals with issues such as your pay plan, travel requirements, geographic location, corporate culture, and much more.

The best sales executives and managers are excellent at "identifying good horse flesh" and then making sure their "course is right for the horse"—there is a perfect fit between the person and this job.

Truth 5: You Can't Lead Where You Won't Go Any More Than You Are Able to Teach the Things You Don't Know

Sales leaders must be willing and capable of handling difficult, demanding, and sensitive issues although it is tantalizingly easier to avoid potentially volatile situations. Unfortunately, being a sales executive or manager can often let you believe that you can do the latter.

Leadership is fundamentally all about setting an example. It is about role modeling and personally exhibiting those characteristics that need to be practiced in the field by salespeople. Specifically, that means getting actively involved with issues such as pricing problems, delivery glitches, calling on difficult customers or prospects, working longer than the required hours, traveling to see difficult-to-get-to locations, resolving conflicts among various constituencies, and a host of other unsavory, distasteful things that fall into the lap of every sales manager in the world.

The fallout that comes from a failure to do those things and abdicating that responsibility is not a pretty sight to see. Ensuing low morale, a lack of respect for you as a sales manager, loss of confidence in management, a perception of hypocrisy, and an overall sense of mistrust for anyone in a management role are all real possibilities that can and do occur.

It takes courage for a sales manager or executive to step up and face the unknown. And here is the fundamental issue: How can you expect salespeople to face the dangers of conflict, refusal, or disagreement if you won't? Sales management is not for the timid or faint of heart.

The second part of this truth is also at the very heart of salesforce performance. Several years ago, we were engaged to work with the U.S. Air Force Reserve Recruiting Command. That organization, so essential to the nation's defense, had experienced difficulty achieving its recruiting targets. Col. Mike Mungavin, commander of the entire operation, knew clearly that it was necessary to get all of their senior recruiters, the military equivalent of sales managers, actively involved. He strongly urged that they:

- Attend required sessions personally.
- Personally participate in each quarterly telecoaching session.
- Log personal time listening to audio programs of our system.
- Work to become certified sales/recruiting professionals in the organization.
- Personally facilitate ongoing training sessions.
- Conduct field audits to evaluate performance.

The results of their personal effort were exemplary. The organization achieved its quota, has exceeded it year after year, and continues to have great results. Much of this success is driven by Colonel Mungavin. He not only "went where others wouldn't go," but also made a Herculean effort to ensure that all sales managers learned, assimilated, and applied knowledge they needed to learn. His zest for superior performance was contagious; his leadership from the front, peerless.

Another example is Air Technologies of Columbus, Ohio, and its vice president of sales, Kurt Lang. Kurt, who has filled in as a regional manager when turnover has occurred, goes into the field and assists salespeople, holds salespeople accountable, exhibits great knowledge about what he has learned, and exhibits great courage, energy, and knowledge when dealing with customers. The results? Exemplary and outstanding sales performance in a tough selling environment where other sales organizations have foundered.

Many years ago, I was personally involved with training more than 20,000 salespeople for a well-known international sales organization. The program that we launched met with only marginal success. After 18 months of intense work, I asked the executive in charge what went wrong. It was extremely revealing when he told me, "We never got the attention of the sales managers . . . they never embraced what we were doing and, as a consequence, the project never took off."

Don't ever believe that anyone in your sales organization will ever get involved if your sales managers don't. If the sales management team doesn't see something as important, no one else will, either.

Truth 6: Salespeople Must Be Hired with Caution, Launched with Clarity, and the Underperforming Ones Replaced with Dispatch

The essence of this rule lies in the speed of hiring and the speed of firing. They both need to move at their own proper speed. The correct speed? Hire more slowly and fire more quickly. In the real world, sales organizations hire too fast and fire too slowly. They have the whole thing backwards. But more about this later.

The reasons for these problems are easy to isolate and identify:

- Not defining a well-coordinated recruiting process.
- Not having a solid, sequential hiring strategy.
- Not applying the right tools in selection.

- A perceived need to fill sales vacancies fast.
- A weak orientation system.
- A poorly designed appraisal system.
- A dysfunctional or nonexistent performance management system.
- No paper trail relative to performance issues.
- Fear of litigation when terminating salespeople.
- Not wanting to hurt someone's feelings.
- A lack of awareness relative to the costs related to keeping poor sales performers too long.
- The eternally optimistic belief that "I can turn this person around."

The underlying reality is that far too many not-so-smart sales organizations are guilty of trying to "sell" candidates into accepting a job offer rather than creating an attractive situation that allows them to be more selective and cautious. This is compounded by poorly communicating clear expectations for the job. Consequently, murky performance issues arise, making exemplary performance difficult to discern from average or subpar results.

When working with a large OEM several years ago, we discovered that their turnover on a national basis hovered at about 41 percent annually. The costs were massive, morale was low, and sales were suffering. Once we installed a process that showed them precisely how to hire with caution and establish clear performance objectives and expectations, they were able to reduce their annual turnover to 19 percent—a 21 percent improvement. The most startling part of this story is that they identified the subpar performers, established new standards for what acceptable performance was, and moved toward a clear-cut system for eliminating those who failed to improve. Most astonishingly, this 21 percent retention improvement was achieved in spite of a stepped-up process for terminating sub-par salespeople. The facts speak for themselves. This improvement also saved them about $12 million in direct and indirect turnover costs.

Truth 7: Pay Plans Are Essential to Sales Performers and Should, Ultimately, Determine How Much of What Gets Sold

Top salespeople enjoy making money. Research shows it, your experience tells you it's true, and there is little doubt that the more closely the compensation is tied to performance, the better that performance will be.

During a recent consulting assignment, a client asked us to evaluate their 45 salespeople. The organization's sales had flattened, profits dissipated, and layoffs were imminent. The most glaring issue we uncovered was that their pay plan, coupled with the experience level of the salesforce, formed a recipe for average or subpar performance.

Their pay plan was an unusually healthy base plus a small bonus based on profitability organizationwide. Each of their salespeople had been with the organization for a number of years, with the average having somewhere around 15 years of service.

The outcome of this scenario should have been predictable. First, most had settled into a comfort zone where each was making in excess of $110,000 per year plus a car, expenses, and full benefit package. They had little desire to work any harder than they needed to maintain the lifestyle they wanted. Their bonus plan was tied to something over which they had no control. How can you pay someone on enterprisewide profitability when they have no input into capital expenditures, office expenses, investments, salaries, marketing costs, and so on? If you do, you breed resentment and eventual complacency. And that's exactly what they did.

The overall sales performance of the group was reflective of this flawed pay plan. What incentive did any of these salespeople have to expend the level of effort required to compete in a highly competitive market? No one had been terminated for years because of poor performance; and the base pay was in no way influenced by performance, was extremely lucrative to begin with, and was coupled with a full array of attractive benefits. The bonus plan was also flawed. No one should have been surprised by the results.

In another situation, salespeople were given a reasonable base and a significant commission based on sales volume and margin on an individual basis. A bonus was based on how successfully each salesperson exceeded his or her personal sales for the previous quarter. There were even additional bonuses for the sale of selected products. The results? You guessed it. Their sustained sales performance far exceeded that of the first sales group.

Let there be little doubt about it: Correctly designed pay plans ultimately drive what happens with a salesforce. A very good friend of mine, a well respected and highly regarded university professor, jokingly puts it this way, "If you pay peanuts, you get monkeys." Intentionally not sophisticated—but correct. Perhaps he could go even further and put it this way, "If you distributed peanuts based on performance, the strongest, fastest, and hungriest monkeys would probably be at the front of the line to get the peanuts!"

Truth 8: Turnover in a Salesforce Is Normal and to Be Expected. Zero Turnover Is Bad, but Too High a Turnover Is Even Worse

Sales organizations, like any other organization made up of human beings, experience personnel changes. With people changing not only jobs, but also entire careers multiple times in their lives, personnel change is to be accepted, anticipated, and factored into the equation.

Too radical a situation at either end of the spectrum, however, is a real cause for concern. Many years ago, a friend of mine was the senior sales officer for an organization with more than 3,000 sales representatives spread across America in the high turnover insurance sales industry where the frequent ebb and flow of salespeople is rampant. This opportunity woke him up to the problems that an 85 percent plus annual turnover can create. One day, one of his sales executives made the statement, "We're not in the insurance business; we're in the recruiting business." My friend's response? "We should be in the selection, training, and retention business . . . that will then allow us to be in the insurance business." And he was right.

Problems of too high a turnover include:

- Poor image among prospects and customers. They ask, "Who's handling my account now?"
- No capacity to provide advanced, meaningful, significant training.
- Little opportunity to develop future senior sales reps and/ or executives or managers from the sales ranks.
- A competitive advantage for your competition.
- Poor image in the marketplace of potential job applicants.
- Low salesperson morale and loyalty.
- Inadequate career planning.
- A constant sense of change, disruption, and lack of continuity.

On the other hand, too little turnover can lead to problems. You need not look any further than to review the example of the organization discussed under Truth 7 to see what can happen when a sales organization is allowed to grow stagnant and have no infusion of new ideas, people, enthusiasm, or energy.

There are far more problems than just flat sales or a lack of growth, including:

- A lack of opportunity for newer or younger salespeople to move into sales territories or positions with greater responsibility.
- Resistance to change, innovation, or learning relative to new products or systems.
- Succession problems relative to moving new salespeople into markets or territories.
- Average or below salespeople who have stayed in sales while their peers have moved on to areas of greater responsibility or a better job. (The great ones leave, and the bad ones stay because they have no place to go.)
- A culture built on shortcuts, complacency, and knowing how to get by rather than get ahead.

What, then, is a healthy turnover? The answer lies in the type of industry in which you find yourself. We have worked in some industries where 20 percent is an acceptable annual turnover figure whereas, in others, 5 percent to 8 percent is more the norm. In the final analysis, benchmarking your turnover numbers versus industry standards may be advisable. However, if you are in an industry with unusually high or low turnover, is there anything that says you must settle for that? I certainly don't think so. Don't you work long and hard to beat the competition? After all, isn't that what sales is all about . . . beating the competition on every front, not just sales? How about in the retention of great salespeople and the planned, intelligent, and purposeful elimination of poor performers?

Truth 9: Sales Executives Must Never Allow Digital Solutions to Dominate a Salesforce's Life, Stifle Creativity, or Curtail Proactivity

Data is critical to sales success. Information that is meaningful and in-depth can often help a salesperson achieve better personal organization, can enhance their sales progress and help them to prospect and sell more effectively. There is example after example of situations where this sort of information has made the difference between winning and losing sales.

There are, however, perhaps just as many cases that prove the opposite to be true. The answer to this dilemma lies in the balance to be found between a sales organization using technology as an aid or allowing it to become an albatross around the neck of proactive salespeople.

Again, like lots of other things, the answer lies in seeking some sort of balance. In determining at what point data entry, learning how to master software, struggling with systems and the resentment of having to do busy work in order to make the system function, actually get in the way of proactive, productive prospecting, face-to-face selling, servicing accounts, and all the other duties that go into a productive sales effort.

We have often heard from clients that their "eyes were bigger than their stomachs" when it came to purchasing sales automation or customer relationship management software. Perhaps they were oversold. Perhaps they overbought. Whatever the cause, they ended up with expensive software that was either never implemented or failed to achieve its full potential. The result? Expensive solutions that never worked, disgruntled salespeople, frustration, and financial loss.

The real answer is to be absolutely sure of several things before you even decide to embark down this potentially slippery path. Here they are:

- How robust does this software really need to be? (Don't buy a guided missile if you only need a pistol.)
- How likely are your salespeople to embrace and even use the software? (Lots of salespeople prefer to sell to people. Not look at a computer screens or bang on keypads.)

- How complex a system will your sales team be able to handle? (Some salespeople have enough trouble with product knowledge, mastering a sales process, self-management and managing a territory. They can't handle another learning hurdle.)
- How effective will your sales management team be at monitoring, managing and reinforcing the system? (Sales managers must champion, understand and manage any system for it to work with any degree of efficiency.)
- How much ongoing support will be required for technical efficiency and ongoing training? (Be sure you have the technical support structure and budget both internally and externally to support whatever system is involved.)

The biggest thing to remember is that "simple and easy-to-use" truly does lie in the eye of the beholder. After more than a quarter of a century of selling and working with salespeople, I have reached one fundamental conclusion. And here it is: Simple really is better. However, what may be simple to one person may not be quite so clear to another. Technology is not bad. In fact, the opposite is true. However, technology is only good if it is used, embraced, and doesn't take away from positive, productive sales time. And achieving that balance is critical.

Truth 10: You Cannot Motivate Salespeople; You Can Only Create an Environment That Rewards the Things They Are Most Motivated by in the First Place

All people are motivated. Unfortunately, some are motivated more than others. Different people are also motivated by different things. The elusive secret so jealously guarded by smart sales organizations is that they hire only the ones who get up every day with great enthusiasm—ready to compete and win within the structure of the organization, what it has to offer, the rewards it provides, the products or services it sells, and the customer base with whom it deals.

I served for a short time as a consultant with a professional athletic team. A vast majority of their players were highly motivated to perform at a peak level of performance. We used assessments that revealed everything that needed to be done to create the precise motivational environment for each player. We laid it out in accurate, exacting terms. In the greatest detail, we explained the most powerful rewards that would appeal to each player; the optimum methods for communicating with each member of the team; how to manage, motivate, and get the best from each player; and other, invaluable data related to each one's attributes, attitude, and values.

One of the coaches fully grasped the concept and used the tools we prescribed. Unfortunately, he wasn't the head coach. The head coach was the one who decided what approach, tools, methods, or systems would be used and which ones wouldn't.

After a period of time, the team failed to perform. Friction grew to epidemic proportion between the head coach and the rest of the team. The assistant coach confided in me that he was often reduced to being the ombudsman between the head coach and the players to keep the two factions at bay by using the tools we had provided. The head coach was eventually fired. Unfortunately, the assistant coach was terminated with him. The assistant coach continues to use the valuable information we provided on a day-to-day basis. The head coach was hired by another team, subsequently fired again, and hasn't had another head coaching job since. The reason? His reputation for alienating players has plagued him his entire coaching career.

Creating the right environment inside of which already motivated people perform is the secret to this whole thing. The process can be divided into three distinct parts:

1. Hiring people who are excited about being part of your organization.
2. Ensuring that what truly does motivate them to perform is present in your organization and in that job.
3. Applying what you know about them to create an environment that empowers them and enables them to perform to their full potential.

It is really that simple. But it is not so easy without the right tools for the selection and identification of only the most highly motivated people, matching the right ones to your environment, identifying the key motivators, and acquiring the knowledge of how to use those tools correctly and the willingness to understand the one, simple truth that people are all motivated by different things. Not every person responds to the same things in the same ways. This might sound like an easy concept to understand. However, the sales landscape is littered with failed sales managers and executives who fell prey to the false belief that all of their salespeople were motivated by the same things that they themselves were or are motivated by. That can be a fatal error. It was for one coach and for many more sales executives. The difference is that sales managers' fates were not spread all over the sports page.

Truth 11: No Salesperson Will Ever Reach Any Level of Meaningful Performance if Expectations Are Not Clearly Established, Communicated, and Verified for Their Acceptance and Total Understanding

It is difficult, if not impossible, for salespeople to perform at a superior level unless they understand the exact expectations that are held for them. People need to know the minimum standards of performance that they are expected to deliver or meet. They also need to know precisely and exactly what *defines* subpar, average, or superior performance. And this relates to far more than just results.

This concept can be misleading for many sales organizations. It is not uncommon for sales managers and executives to assign sales quotas without defining the exact performance parameters to be met along the way. This is running a sales organization by end-result expectations rather than by in-process expectations. And there is a big difference between the two. By the same token, simply assigning someone a sales quota is a big enough mistake on its own. When told what to do, people never take ownership. However, when *they* tell you what *they* can do, *they* will do all in their power to achieve it, particularly if it is in writing and made public knowledge.

Meaningful standards of performance far exceed the simple metric of achieving a sales quota. Although these nonsales-specific standards are elusive for some organizations to grasp, they are far more valuable than trying to measure performance by simple sales volume alone. They deal, instead, with standards relative to specific behaviors, values that the job rewards, attitudes to exhibit, attributes to be delivered, skills to be honed, and standards to be met on a day-to-day, week-to-week, month-by-month basis.

Measurement should take the form of an effective performance management and feedback system—one that ensures that salespeople know the exact standards of performance that are expected and monitors them to ensure that these standards are met, achieved, or surpassed. Initiate a process like this and achievement of sales quotas generally follows. If not, a course correction needs to be made. If shortfalls occur relative to acceptable standards, there are consequences—not at the end of the quarter or year when sales results are computed, but now when you can influence the eventual outcome.

It is not unusual for sales organizations to have no exacting job descriptions, standards of performance, performance objectives, appraisal systems, or anything of the like in place for their sales teams. They judge the effectiveness of a salesperson or entire salesforce by the sales results they deliver—and too late, too.

Unfortunately, their logic is often flawed because of the disparity of sales potential that lies between territories, economic fluctuations between markets, territories and customers, and so on. By the same token, there are some organizations that are so systemically driven that everyone is busy filling out forms, evaluating performance, and meeting for the sake of meeting that nothing else ever happens, including sales. Like everything in life, there needs to be a balance.

Truth 12: Performance Counts in Sales . . . but It Is Accountability That Really Pays

Accountability simply means being held answerable for your own actions and results. There is much more about this later in the book. At this point, it is essential to understand that if sales leaders, managers, or executives wait until performance reports are in, it is too late. The game is over.

Instead, it is better to create two simultaneous scenarios. First, you must create a culture that says people must be willing and freely accepting of the premise that they, alone, are answerable for their own successes and failures. In the absence of that culture, your organization will be fraught with finger pointing, denial, backstabbing, blaming, and organization-wide deceit.

Perhaps the best example of this goes way back to my days as a college football player. I was a lineman and played offensive guard. If I missed a block or blew an assignment, I knew it, the coaches knew it, my teammates knew it, and a careful eye in the stands knew it. Eventually the films (now video) would show it, too. So there was no finger pointing or denial. By the same token, if I held illegally, I caused the 15-yard penalty. I was caught, fair and square, under the rules. In the NFL, the official even publicly announces the number of the offender. That's accountability—often on national television.

If you haven't forged to have this type of culture within your sales team, you will never get to the real issues relative to a salesperson's willingness to avoid denial, blame, or the shifting of mistakes to someone else. Everything will be someone else's fault.

Second, you must have a system in place for holding people accountable (more about that later, too). If you don't have a system for accountability and some form of performance management in place that evaluates factors other than pure sales results, you will never be able to hold someone accountable for issues that ultimately determine a person's sales success or failure.

Each of these Universal Truths can be applied to any organization anywhere in the world. It makes no difference whether your organization is large or small, national or international, or whether you sell products or services business to business or business to consumer.

A principle, unlike a technique, is something that is universal in its application. For example, who could argue with "Treat others as you yourself would like to be treated" or "Every journey begins with the first step." Principles are all about the whys behind the whats and hows. And all of these truths are based on principles. That is what makes them so powerful and valuable. Learn them and use them. They could make both you and your organization smarter, better, and probably even more profitable. How about *much* more profitable?

CHAPTER 2
THE SUPERIOR SELLING CHAPTER REVIEW

- Unfortunately, sales management and leadership has, all too often, been the recipient of either high-handed philosophies or a grab bag of disjointed techniques.

- The result has been a series of maneuvers, tricks, or tactics.
- Universal truths are principles that can guide a smart sales organization to greatness. The 12 truths are:

Truth 1: A sales organization will never be any stronger than the salespeople who are recruited, selected, and hired to be a part of it.

Truth 2: Invest your time where it counts: with the best performing salespeople and with those who hold the greatest potential.

Truth 3: A sales organization cannot be led from behind a desk.

Truth 4: The best sales executives and sales managers are the most skilled at judging talent and placing the right people in the right place.

Truth 5: You can't lead where you won't go any more than you are able to teach things you don't know.

Truth 6: Salespeople must be hired with caution, launched with clarity, and the underperforming ones replaced with dispatch.

Truth 7: Pay plans are essential to sales performance and should, ultimately, determine how much of what gets sold.

Truth 8: Turnover in a salesforce is normal and to be expected. No turnover is bad, but too high a turnover is even worse.

Truth 9: Sales executives must never allow digital solutions to dominate a salesforce's life, stifle creativity, or curtail proactivity.

Truth 10: You cannot motivate salespeople; you can only create an environment wherein they motivate themselves.

Truth 11: No salesperson will ever perform to any meaningful level if expectations are not clearly established, communicated, and verified for acceptance and understanding.

Truth 12: Performance counts in sales . . . but it is accountability that really pays.

Hiring and Retaining Great Salespeople

The First Step Is the Most Important

As we've discussed, it's an old but proven principle. Success in any venture does start with a first step. But that first step for sales organizations can sometimes be a misstep because of confusion that can lead to a disastrous journey right out of the box. For some, that misstep is falsely believing a larger marketing budget is the only answer; for others, it is the belief that a new or repackaged product will win the day. Some believe that a new commission plan or contest enticing salespeople to sell a certain product will be the next, instant answer to their sales success.

The answer is not found in any one of these by itself. Even the greatest plan, no matter what strategy, can fall apart without great execution. And execution of even a mediocre plan can be made great with one single ingredient: the right people in the right place doing the right things. It's that simple.

Several years ago, an organization came to us because they were experiencing difficulty year after year in achieving their sales plan. In fact, they had not reached their revenue target for five successive years. Something drastic was needed. They initiated a four-part strategy that allowed them to:

1. Quadruple their marketing budget.
2. Invest in ongoing, meaningful sales and sales management training.
3. Initiate a plan to hire more salespeople—while absolutely ensuring that only the right people were hired.
4. Systematically and rigorously evaluate all existing performers to determine their capacity to perform and assess how well they would fit long term within the new, demanding culture. The organization then replaced those who didn't fit and developed a more significant reward system for those who did.

Another one of our clients has been successful in launching a joint venture with a major retailer. Their concept is to have ministores located inside retailers' stores selling logo wear to businesses who shop at the stores. They have a full line of products, including shirts, sweaters, caps, golf wear, and hundreds of other items that appeal to smaller business employees who regularly visit the stores for office and business supplies. It is a brilliant strategy designed to reach an underserviced market in a very direct way.

Our client's CEO knew there was one initial ingredient essential for the plan to work: the right people. We assisted in the process of selecting those right salespeople—ones who, frankly, could pass a rather demanding muster and prove to all three of us—our client, the retailer, and us—that they could perform.

We recommended that the client accept about one in five applicants that we saw. The executives at both the client and retailer knew that the going would be tough and sometimes slower than hoped for because there was a rigorous store opening schedule. The most interesting part of this project is to hypothesize about the success of the venture if the four of five rejected had been hired. Frankly, I don't want to think about it. But I do know this. Several executives told us that in their traditional hiring model, they would have hired four of every five.

Your Challenge

The single biggest challenge to this approach is one that is both logical and emotional in nature. The logical part of the argument is that having someone in place is better than having no one at all. This, however, is a false argument when you consider the downside of having the wrong salesperson in place, for example:

- Wasted leads and lost opportunities.
- Customer and prospect alienation.
- Loss of goodwill in the marketplace.
- Poor image and reputation.
- Morale problems caused for other salespeople.
- Lost time and energy in hiring, training, and managing.
- Delivery and customer service problems.
- Cost related to hiring and rehiring.
- Costs related to turnover.

The emotional side of the argument lies in the danger of hiring someone you personally like regardless of their proven level of competency. Couple this with the often-used mirror test (the old method of simply being able to fog a mirror and you have the job) and you can imagine the problems.

Having the right people in the right jobs is the essence of organizational performance. In the world of the twenty-first century sales, it is, perhaps, the most critical ingredient for success because of the murderous competition in place, which promises to only get worse.

The Five Most Important Questions

Literally thousands of assessments are available that purport to measure a salesperson's capacity to perform. Some are complex; others are simple. A vast majority are some form of thinly veiled behavior or personality assessment that purport to explain how one personality type or another is a better fit for sales. Answering that single question, however, is just not enough.

We have been assisting organizations worldwide in selecting salespeople for more than 20 years. And in that time period, we have seen trends come and go. We have a unique approach that has allowed us to retain accounts for 10 to 15 years. And we have done so in a very low-key way without expending one nickel on marketing, advertising, or promotion.

This success has been driven by providing exacting answers to these five questions:

1. *Why* would this person be interested in selling as a career in the first place?
2. *Will* this person actually sell?
3. *How* will this person choose to sell?
4. *Can* this person access the skills required to sell?
5. How effectively will this person deliver all four of these capacities to be able to sell *here* in this unique, one-of-a-kind sales position?

It is only when you have definitive answers to these five questions that you can even begin to determine if you are hiring the right person (more about that later).

The Fatal Flaw in Selection

As we have discussed, many sales organizations and sales executives believe that prior experience in an industry, a specific marketplace, or with a certain product is the main reason for hiring or not hiring a salesperson. That is just not accurate thinking. It is, instead, being held hostage by a false premise.

There are many reasons why this premise is simply not true, for example:

- A presumption that the person's previous industry experience was a positive, productive one.
- An assumption that the person in question possesses a high level of motivation, drive, and selling skills.
- A belief that the person is available because of circumstances over which he or she had no control (downsizing, etc.) rather than because of average or below performance.

The breakdown of capacities that drive sales performance is shown in Figure 3.1.

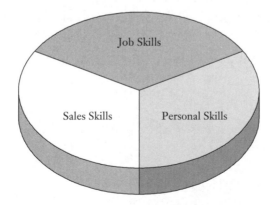

FIGURE 3.1 Job, Sales, Personal Skills Model

- Job Skills: Product and marketplace knowledge to include experience in an industry.

- Sales Skills: Those capacities related to a person's capacity to understand and apply state-of-the-art selling skills relative to appropriate level prospecting, selling, and account management functions.

- Personal Skills: Those individual capacities that determine a person's ability to implement the job and sales skills they possess—attributes such as self-starting capacity, self-management, personal motivation, consistency, and literally scores of other, essential skills.

Job, product, or marketplace knowledge is only one-third of what is required, whereas sales and personal skills comprise a full two-thirds. However, it is even more dramatic than that. Over the years, we have developed this formula:

$$\left(\text{Job Skills} + \text{Sales Skills}\right) \times \frac{\text{Personal}}{\text{Skills}} = \frac{\text{Sales Performance}}{\text{Quotient}}$$

Let's look at an example with a 1 to 10 scale, with 10 being excellent and 1 being poor. In this case, you have a candidate with extensive product, industry, and marketplace experience. You give that person a score of 10 on job skills. That same person, however, has sales skills of 5 and personal skills of only 4. Here is what that person looks like in our formula:

$$(10 + 5) \times 4 = 60$$

Another person has job skills of only a 3, sales skills are 8, and personal skills are 9:

$$(3 + 8) \times 9 = 99$$

Personal skills are the multiplier of performance. Product knowledge, job, or sales skills are things that can be taught, learned, or acquired. Sales skills can be learned intellectually and eventually honed through experience and face-to-face inter-action with large numbers of prospects and customers and in-the-field coaching. Personal skills are a unique combination of personal attributes, values, talents, and experience. They, too, can be learned, coached, mentored, taught, and honed through in-depth experience. However, the capacity to identify some-one's fundamental predisposition to possess these characteristics is where the magic comes in.

The good news is that sales skills and personal skills can both be measured and assessed. That is especially good news because they are the real drivers of personal performance on an in-dividual-by-individual basis.

The Right Stuff

Having the right stuff is a function of a more refined diagram (see Figure 3.2).

The most fundamental question of the five is the one that asks "Why?" In essence, why would anyone ever choose to sell

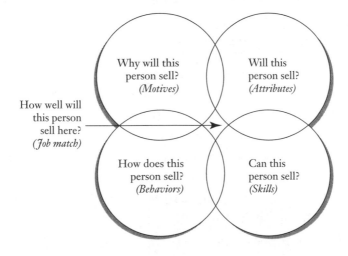

FIGURE 3.2 **Why, Will, How, Can, How Well Circles**

in the first place? The answer to that question is the most basic of all issues that drive human performance toward any venture or undertaking. It is a question of motive as driven by a person's interests and values.

In the final analysis, the why behind choices is often the primary driver of performance. Why does a human being choose to do anything, whether serve in the military, be a teacher, join a religious order, or become a salesperson? The answer lies in what that person values most. It also lies in whether what the person values most is rewarded in his or her unique environment. If there is a match between the person's dominant values and the organization, there is a match. It is an even stronger match if those exact things are rewarded by the particular job. Unfortunately, for most organizations, that sophisticated match is often overlooked or not recognized at all.

My close friend and colleague, Bill Bonnstetter, CEO of Target Training International, has conducted extensive research into this whole notion of motives and performance for many years. According to his model, there are six basic values or motives that drive human beings. His research is long, in-depth, high quality, exceedingly persuasive, and has proven to be extremely accurate in terms of sophisticated validation studies conducted over years and years.

Bonnstetter's values are:

- *Theoretical*: An interest in and need for learning for the sake of learning. It is further defined as having a need to master subjects, topics, or areas of interest.
- *Utilitarian/Economic*: A need for financial gain, practicality of thought, and a sense of measuring your self-worth in terms of that financial gain.
- *Social*: The need to help others even if faced with personal loss to accomplish this end.
- *Individualistic/Political*: A strong predisposition to control your own destiny and the destiny of others.

- *Aesthetic:* An appreciation of beauty, nature, the environment, harmony, and pleasant surroundings.
- *Traditional/Regulatory:* Interest in rules, a standard of performance, behavior, and the need for an external system of living to define that behavior.

Bonnstetter goes on to say that the ranking of these values will define, in great measure, the interest—or lack of it—in ventures or environments that reward those values.

For example, if a position rewards study, research, and in-depth knowledge, a person who values this sort of activity would be highly interested, engaged, and potentially well suited. By the same token, if a person is not interested in intellectual activity, the position in question may likely not be a good fit. For example, a repetitive, simple sale being made to a rather unsophisticated customer base may not appeal to a person who values—and is interested in—higher level, intellectually demanding thought. On the contrary, a person who does not enjoy learning, studying, and being intellectually challenged may not flourish in an environment that demands a great deal of thought-stimulating activity and ongoing learning.

Bonnstetter's research got even more interesting when he studied 178 top-ranked salespeople from 178 different organizations in both the United States and Germany. These people were not second best or also-rans. Instead, all were the best that their individual organizations had to offer.

The results? Close to 80 percent had utilitarian/economic valuing as their number one value. These people valued financial gain, measured their personal self-worth in terms of financial gain, were practical in their thoughts, and sought a profession that valued and rewarded financial gain, which meant:

- The organizations rewarded superior performance with financial remuneration and had hired those types of people.

- The organizations that reward this value could be one step closer to identifying their potentially top performers if they can measure this capacity in the hiring process.
- True sales organizations must be sure to continue to reward top performers and meet all commitments so they keep those top performers.

What does all of this really mean? Simply that valuing something strongly means that those are the things you care about most deeply and passionately. A low valuing means that you don't care about those things at all. If people are in jobs that reward things they are most passionate about, they will work long, hard, and in a committed, dedicated way—everyday. If they are in jobs that do not reward, or perhaps even punish those values and interests, the opposite occurs.

Think about these examples. Imagine a low theoretical person as a university professor or researcher. Imagine a low traditional/regulatory person in the Marines or a low social person as a social worker. How about a highly utilitarian/economic person in a job that has a low, fixed salary or a high aesthetic person in a job that punishes creative expression.

The pattern is clear. These interests and values are the *why* behind someone's motives to perform. What does this mean to you? Let's look at a few more examples:

Sales Position A—A highly structured job where customer service is more important than sales. The pay plan is a base salary only with no bonus or commission. The position requires someone to sell traditional, old-line, and simple-to-understand and explain products to fairly unsophisticated, middle-to-low income customers.

Strong candidate: Theoretical—low.
*   Utilitarian/Economic—low.*
*   Social—high.*
*   Individualistic/Political—low.*
*   Traditional/Regulatory—high.*

Sales Position B—A straight commission job that requires a transactional, direct, and strong closing sales approach. The product is simple with no customer service required. However, there are very strict rules to follow on legal issues, compliance, and warranty administration.

Strong candidate: *Theoretical—low.*
                         Utilitarian/Economic—high.
                         Social—low.
                         Individualistic/Political—high.
                         Traditional/Regulatory—high.

Let's look at a position that requires salespeople to regularly interact with senior-level, highly educated prospects and customers who are seeking solid answers to tough questions. This job carries a modest base with commission and a bonus that drives the income to a solid six figures. The job further requires salespeople to find conquest accounts and win them in the face of highly competitive factors.

How would a low theoretical, low utilitarian/economic, or low individualistic/political person perform in this environment? This type of job would be all wrong for that person. This does not mean that the person would not be ideally suited for another position in the organization. However, this particular job requires and rewards someone who is strongly theoretical and enjoys learning, is driven by financial gain, and wants to control his or her own destiny along with that of others.

If this person's values are not known and reviewed, discussed, and compared against what is rewarded, valued, and held in high esteem for that particular job, the outcome is potentially disastrous for both the candidate and the organization. Yet, virtually all sales organizations fail to deal with the critical issue of values, interests, and motives when they hire salespeople. They overlook the fundamental *why* of performance altogether.

The combinations are endless. Here, however, is the bottom line. We see very few organizations that match the job's unique reward hierarchy and/or the person's motives to determine the most fundamental questions of all: Why would someone be attracted to a specific sales position in the first place, and how passionate will that person be about performing the job on a day-to-day basis?

We recently evaluated a sales position with our comparison tool, TriMetrix™, which is designed to evaluate motives along with all the other key job factors. TriMetrix provides unparalleled, accurate data relative to compatibility between people and jobs. It first benchmarks the job, then the people. Most organizations have it all wrong; they benchmark their top performers. The secret is to benchmark the job first. Then benchmark people against the job. We examine this whole notion later in this chapter.

It could be argued that values, interests, and motives are at the very core of a person's passion for life and that they dictate a person's fundamental thoughts, actions, attitudes, behaviors, and performance. If you want to prove this concept, simply get into a discussion with someone about something he or she values or cares about deeply and watch the sparks fly, for example:

- Education.
- Politics.
- Religion.
- Funding the arts.
- Following rules.
- Money.
- Power.
- Control.
- The environment.
- Welfare.

All of these issues can be potentially volatile because they are all things that people feel passionately about. Although there may be one or two issues that are relatively meaningless to a person (the person is around the mean score on that issue), there are others about which that person passionately feels (high score) or totally deplores (low score). And, surprisingly, we have discovered that people are just as passionate about what they deplore as about what they love. For example, the phrase "people with lots of money are never happy" was probably first uttered by a low economic person!

The most fundamental issue is simply: Values, motives, and interests are the things that fuel a person's passions. Unfortunately, far too many people find little passion in what they do on the job. Therefore, they go elsewhere to have it fueled. Whether it is to spend time on a hobby, start a part-time job, join a club, get involved with a religious group, or start a part-time business, the result is the same. Their attention and passionate performance is directed away from the job and on to something else.

Imagine the power of having someone in a job that totally fuels his or her passion—a job that allows daily immersion in issues that he or she cares deeply and passionately about, a job that rewards his or her real interests. That is the very power of values, motives, and interests and the most universally overlooked factor when hiring sales champions. But get ready—that is only one of the missing pieces that virtually all organizations and sales executives miss. And those missing pieces are the things that cause low morale, turnover, and poor performance.

Will a Person Sell?

Wanting to do something, then doing it, and ultimately doing it well are three very different issues. In literally thousands of cases, we have seen salespeople whose values 100 percent matched the values and motives that were demanded and rewarded by their job. They were legitimately fueled by the exact things that the job rewarded. They were there for the right reasons. They legitimately wanted to be doing the job. Unfortunately, we saw a vast number of people who did not perform despite their heartfelt intention. What does that say? That motives, alone, are not sufficient as indicators of performance. Motives are the base—the why of performance. Without them, the passion is never there. And passion is the thing that sustains peak performance. However, another series of questions starts with the question, "Will this person sell?" and deals with someone's fundamental capacity to deliver what the job demands.

This factor deals with a person's willingness and starts with a set of attributes—attributes that are driven by how a person's brain functions relative to the deliverable capacities that a specific job requires, such as self-starting, goal-directedness, handling rejection, and more. It is the clarity and focus that a person has, can build on, and sustain relative to those attributes that drive a person's fundamental capacity to perform in a specific job on a long-term basis.

Our tool, TriMetrix, accomplishes this goal with great accuracy. TriMetrix is several tools combined into one. It incorporates the motives that the job rewards, the attributes it requires, and the behaviors that the job demands into a straightforward benchmark for hiring and performance management.

TriMetrix allows us to benchmark the job in unique ways. For example, my associate, Bill Bonnstetter has a unique perspective. We referred earlier to the false logic that he exposed.

Most organizations falsely believe that they can benchmark a position by identifying their top sales performers and then attempting to clone them with new hires.

Here is the error of their logic, according to Bonnstetter. What if you are managing a major league baseball team, but your roster is full of minor league level players? If you benchmarked your top players, you'd likely be establishing a subpar bench-mark, wouldn't you?

By the same token, it is not unusual to see that absolute, top performers are virtually uncloneable anyway. How many Ted Williamses, Willie Mayses, Mickey Mantles, or Sammy Sosas are there? Bonnstetter suggests that you ask yourself the simple question, "If the job could tell us what it demands for successful performance in it, what would it tell us?"

Together, we have developed a process that allows us to have key stakeholders score the position by answering a series of 92 questions related to the necessary attributes the job requires, 24 related to the motives it rewards, and 14 that deal with the job's necessary behaviors. We then digitally compile the top seven attributes, top three values and interests, and top three behaviors that successfully fulfill the job demands. Candidates then score a companion, three-part assessment that compares them to the job.

Let's look at a recent sales position that we completed for a client. In terms of attributes, the top seven were, in order:

1. Results orientation.
2. Continuous learning.
3. Self-management.
4. Self-starting.
5. Goal achievement.
6. Resiliency.
7. Flexibility.

We also scored a very different position, a lead software developer position in a high-tech firm. The top attributes for that job were:

1. Self-management.
2. Problem solving.

3. Continuous learning.

4. Results orientation.

5. Personal accountability.

6. Leading others.

7. Accountability for others.

Note that although three of the attributes are the same (results orientation, continuous learning, and self-management), they are not in the same order whereas four of the attributes for the two jobs are very different. Why is that? Because they are very different jobs!

Let's look at a sales management position, also from our archives of scored positions:

1. Developing others.

2. Teamwork.

3. Diplomacy and tact.

4. Self-management.

5. Planning and organizing.

6. Goal achievement.

7. Influencing others.

We have three jobs each requiring different attributes with some of the same attributes in common but in different order. Note that self-management appears in each job. Self-management is, by our definition, the ability to prioritize and complete tasks in order to deliver desired outcomes within allotted time frames. It is also independently pursuing objectives in an organized and efficient manner, prioritizing tasks and activities, meeting work flow requirements without direct supervision, and minimizing work flow disruptions and time wasters to complete high-quality work within a prescribed time frame. Can you think of many professional-level jobs that don't require some degree of self-management? That's precisely why this single attribute appears somewhere in the top five of virtually any professional level job we score.

In all, we evaluate 23 attributes that are universal across all jobs:

1. Self-starting.
2. Goal achievement.
3. Customer focus.
4. Empathetic outlook.
5. Objective listening.
6. Influencing others.
7. Leading others.
8. Continuous learning.
9. Planning and organization.
10. Developing others.
11. Flexibility.
12. Results orientation.
13. Conceptual thinking.
14. Resiliency.
15. Decision making.
16. Teamwork.
17. Problem solving.
18. Personal accountability.
19. Diplomacy and tact.
20. Self-management.
21. Conflict management.
22. Interpersonal skills.
23. Accountability for others.

Let's revisit the values, motives, and interests side of the equation. Let's look at what these different jobs rewarded. We call this the Rewards/Culture Feedback Section of the TriMetrix.

Sales Position	Lead Software Developer Position	Sales Manager Position
Utilitarian/Economic	Theoretical	Utilitarian/Economic
Individualistic/Political	Traditional/Regulatory	Individualistic/Political
Theoretical	Individualistic/Political	Theoretical

Now, for good measure, let's look at a very different job from our archived TriMetrix evaluations. It is an administrative support job, a clerical job that supports a sales team:

Attributes	Values and Interests
Results Orientation	Utilitarian/Economic
Conceptual Thinking	Traditional/Regulatory
Problem Solving	Theoretical
Taking Responsibility	
Empathetic Outlook	
Teamwork	

This job requires a strong capacity to deliver results, the ability to think in unconventional ways, good problem-solving skills, and assuming responsibility for the support of the sales team. It also requires the empathy to understand what salespeople deal with and the ability to be a productive team member. The job rewards someone who knows that the job is all about generating revenue and not just paper pushing. However, it also requires following the rules relative to policies, procedures, and protocol and demands that someone be willing to learn new ideas.

This is a very different job from the sales position that rewards two of the same things (economic gain and learning new concepts) yet requires very different attributes. The sales and sales support jobs are in the same organization. What does that say? That the culture of the organization is clear. The organization is in business to make money but rewards innovation, creative thinking, and requires people to learn and embrace new ideas.

The sales position in this organization requires someone who can deliver results, not just promises or processes. It requires a person who will learn, can manage himself or herself, will be a self-starter, and will work to achieve clear goals. It also requires resiliency and flexibility.

Not every person is suited for every job. And not every salesperson is suited for every sales job. If you're going to invest the time, energy, resources, and confidence in someone, it is essential to have the right person for your job.

We have not yet discussed personality or behavior. We have, instead, discussed only motives and interests along with personal attributes. Again, remember that attributes are a function of a person's clarity and focus, which is essentially the degree to which the person is able to discern patterns while sustaining a targeted level of attention. It is, essentially, how someone's brain works.

And all of this is scientific, measurable, and accurate. After seeing thousands of assessments, we suggest that the major difference between those who perform well and those who don't often lies in the attribute area. Yet, this is another area that is overlooked and rarely measured. This area is the single capacity that empowers a person to perform or not perform. It's just that basic.

To complete the puzzle, we take a look at behavior. But let me caution you here. In our process, the attributes and motives or interests are far more important than behavior. In many circles, however, that could be a minority view. Here's how it works, again:

1. Motives and interests—Why would someone do a job in the first place?
2. Attributes—Will this person do the job?

3. Behavior—How will this person do the job?

4. Skills—Can this person do the job?

5. Job Match—To what degree does this person have the motives (interests), attributes (clarity and focus), personality (behavior), and skill sets (skills) that this specific job requires?

Let's examine behaviors. TriMetrix evaluates eight specific behavioral outcomes that a job would require:

1. Competitiveness.

2. Urgency.

3. Frequent change.

4. Flexibility.

5. Customer oriented.

6. Frequent interaction with others.

7. Organized workplace.

8. Analysis of data.

Let's now compare the behaviors that each of the jobs we have already discussed require:

Sales	Sales Management	Lead Software Developer	Admin. Support
Competitiveness	Urgency	Analysis of data	Analysis of data
Urgency	Frequent change	Competitiveness	Organized workplace
Frequent interaction with others	Competitiveness	Flexibility	Customer oriented

This means that each job is slightly different. However, the sales job was much faster paced, required higher energy, and was more interpersonally demanding than, for example, either the administrative support or lead software jobs. Both the sales and sales management jobs require similar behaviors. However, the sales job requires more frequent interaction with others whereas the sales management job requires the capacity to deal with frequent change. But that's common sense, isn't it?

And therein lies the problem. Personalities or behaviors are easy to spot, simple to understand, and clearly above the surface. Attributes, interests, and motives are not. And, in the long run, these are the more essential factors that ultimately determine success or failure for most people in most jobs, including sales or sales management.

You must take time to hire with caution and look far beyond the obvious. You don't need to be told the horrible cost that goes with hiring the wrong salesperson. You need to proceed with caution and hire only those who match the exact parameters of what you are looking for. In fact, a strong argument could be made that even expending *any* time, energy, or training dollars on the wrong people often proves to be a monumental waste of resources.

Several years ago, we developed a selling skills assessment that has been translated into a number of languages and distributed worldwide. It has proven its versatility in thousands of organizations and truly does measure a person's complex selling skills for selling in today's competitive world. That completes the picture. However, we have seen something interesting through analyzing tens of thousands of these assessments as well. Most salespeople have a reasonable level of selling skill. Most, however, don't have a systematic, consistent way of implementing it. In short, they don't have a repeatable sales process. And if they do, no one goes into the field to help them apply it with greater skill.

Hiring great salespeople is essential. But you need to hire only those who fit the parameters of your sales position. It is the most fundamental building block of all. However, it doesn't stop there. It just starts the process.

CHAPTER 3

THE SUPERIOR SELLING CHAPTER REVIEW

■ The most fundamental sales success principle is to have only the right salespeople in place.

■ Successful sales performance is far more than determining whether a person has the personality to sell.

■ There are five questions you need to ask about sales candidates' capacity to perform:

1. Why would this person be interested in selling as a career?

2. Will this person actually sell?

3. How will this person choose to sell?

4. Can this person access the skills required to sell?

5. How well will this person deliver all four of the capacities to be able to sell here in this unique, one-of-a-kind environment?

■ Previous industry experience is far overblown as being the primary requirement for the selection of salespeople.

■ The Sales Performance Quotient reveals a person's capacity to perform:

$$(\text{Job Skills} + \text{Sales Skills}) \times \frac{\text{Personal}}{\text{Skills}} = \frac{\text{Sales Performance}}{\text{Quotient}}$$

■ Personal skills are the multiplier of performance.

■ The why of performance serves as the central source for achievement—it is the role that a person's primary motives play in performance.

■ People are driven by one or several of the following interests or values:

Theoretical.

Utilitarian/economic.

Social.

Individualistic/political.

Aesthetic.

Traditional/regulatory.

- Those things that someone values and cares about are sources of motivation for that person.
- Benchmarking jobs instead of the top performers in them is essential to being able to understand what a specific job requires of successful candidates.
- Don't be tempted to benchmark only top performers. Instead, answer what the job itself requires for successful performance.
- The degree of clarity and focus that people have on a concept that their job requires ultimately defines their ability to perform on a consistent basis.
- Different jobs require different attributes for successful performance. The 23 attributes are:

Attribute 1: Self-starting.

Attribute 2: Goal achievement.

Attribute 3: Customer focus.

Attribute 4: Empathetic outlook.

Attribute 5: Objective listening.

Attribute 6: Influencing others.

Attribute 7: Leading others.

Attribute 8: Continuous learning.

Attribute 9: Planning and organization.

Attribute 10: Developing others.

Attribute 11: Flexibility.

Attribute 12: Results orientation.

Attribute 13: Conceptual thinking.

Attribute 14: Resiliency.

Attribute 15: Decision making.

Attribute 16: Teamwork.

Attribute 17: Problem solving.

Attribute 18: Personal accountability.

Attribute 19: Diplomacy and tact.

Attribute 20: Self-management.

Attribute 21: Conflict management.

Attribute 22: Interpersonal skills.

Attribute 23: Accountability for others.

- Most professional positions, like sales jobs, require self-management skills.
- Behaviors vary from job to job. These behaviors are:

Behavior 1: Urgency.

Behavior 2: Competitiveness.

Behavior 3: Frequent change.

Behavior 4: Versatility.

Behavior 5: Frequent interaction with others.

Behavior 6: Organized workplace.

Behavior 7: Customer oriented.

Behavior 8: Analysis of data.

- Successful job fit means matching a person's values, attributes, behaviors, and skills to that which the job requires.
- Although selling skills are essential, they are the least important. Selling skills can be taught and learned by someone whose interests, passions, attributes, and behavior match the job requirements.

Selecting and Empowering the Right Sales Managers

Great Leadership Equals Great Sales Performance

Even with great salespeople in place, no sales organization will perform any better than the quality of leadership, coaching, mentoring, and direction than it receives. In the final analysis, it is the quality of sales management that ultimately determines the quality of the sales organization and its long-term performance.

Unlike other functions where there is a prescribed set of protocols or systems to be followed and a predictable outcome that can be achieved with great accuracy, sales managers, executives, or leaders are dealing with a multitude of elusive variables that ultimately determine the success or failure of the sales enterprise. It is not a production line, manufacturing facility, or the like. Instead, it deals with slippery variables related to elusive predictions, varying levels of skill among salespeople, unpredictable outcomes, varying economic conditions, changing buying cycles, budgets, mergers, acquisitions, and much more.

These multiple variables all have one common denominator that makes the sales arena very different from any other environment: Sales is driven by the human factor in 100 percent of the cases. And like any uniquely human venture, it incorporates elements of psychology, social psychology, anthropology, sociology, learning theory, educational psychology, and myriad other social science variables that can, and do, enter the picture. Orchestrating all of these disciplines can often be as much an art as it is a science. Unfortunately, many of these disciplines are subjects that woefully few sales executives have studied or, at least, have studied recently. These are the fundamental factors that fuel the engine of any sales endeavor.

Compound this with the duties of handling personnel issues, implementing marketing strategies, monitoring pay plans, coordinating travel requirements, planning, scheduling, enhancing product knowledge, providing marketplace knowledge, ordering, having customer interface, performing administrative duties, and juggling bureaucratic demands, and the difficult role that defines effective sales leadership should be clear.

Because sales organizations have so much riding on the performance of their sales managers, they cannot afford to be haphazard in the selection and retention of people for such essential leadership slots. Another harsh reality? Too many sales organizations *are* too haphazard. They just don't take the time and energy required to be sure that they have the most qualified and capable people filling this essential role.

For example, Frank Chamberlain, a close friend and colleague, puts it this way: "A-level players hire A players, B players hire C players, and C players hire D players." The former CEO of a high-tech firm, Frank saw this firsthand. Are you an A, B, or C player?

Strong Sales Performance Isn't an Indicator of Sales Management Potential

Perhaps the most common error made by organizations is the aforementioned tendency to promote a strong sales performer into a sales management role. We have clearly established that these are two different jobs, requiring very different talents and skills. However, this is such an obscenely repeated error that it needs to be revisited.

In some cases, the salesperson who is appointed sales manager is the last one standing after the smoke has cleared. In organizations with high turnover, this is far more common than in ones with a lower loss of personnel. However, with those having lower turnover, it may not be the last one standing who becomes the sales manager, but the one with the most tenure or highest sales volume. Unfortunately, neither of these scenarios necessarily yields the best candidates for this difficult, demanding job, either.

Reasons for this false logic include these five:

1. The belief that superior sales skills automatically translate into superior sales management skills.

2. A reluctance to place someone into the sales management position who has not proven his or her sales mettle to the sales team he or she will lead.

3. An assumption that unless someone has been the number one salesperson, the sales team will not respect or follow that person.

4. The belief that every salesperson wants to move into sales management.

5. The contention that industry experience coupled with field sales experience automatically qualifies someone for a sales management position.

When a highly successful salesperson is taken from the field and placed into a sales management position, two potentially bad things can occur. First, the organization loses the productivity of a top sales professional. Second, there is often an unwilling or unqualified sales manager in place. Unfortunately, there are circumstances where both occur. And that's a real disaster.

Although either or both of these situations do not always occur, they do occur far more often than they should. The two jobs require very different sets of attributes. In the previous chapter, we provided samples of jobs to determine the differences between the fundamental attributes required for two sales and sales management positions. Not surprisingly, the top three were very different:

Sales	Sales Management
Results Orientation	Developing Others
Continuous Learning	Teamwork
Self-Management	Diplomacy and Tact

The two jobs required two different types of people with differing attributes. Sales was far more geared toward personal performance while sales management was more geared toward the development of others, the team, and organization. But all of this is common sense, isn't it? So what is the challenge? Unfortunately, common sense doesn't always rule when it comes to endeavors involving people, feelings, emotions, egos, income, and personal gain. In addition, most organizations don't really know how to benchmark the job and then measure the correct attributes that the job requires in any clear, precise way.

It should come as no surprise that just as rigorous a screening process should be conducted for sales management or sales executive positions as is demanded for sales positions. It could even be argued that sales management or executive screening should be even more rigorous. This may be distressing to some because so many promotions to sales management positions historically come from within. However, this is such a critical hiring decision that you probably need to reconsider whether this self-limiting internal promotion theory should really be your standard.

It is not necessarily a good practice to establish an expectation that the next career move for a salesperson is an automatic promotion to sales management just as it is not a great idea to establish a culture that says there should be an automatic move from being a sales manager to being a sales executive, president, or CEO. There are many fundamental reasons to avoid this trap, for example:

- The available talent pool for sales management positions is significantly reduced if you solely or primarily promote from within.
- Political infighting becomes the rule of the day as salespeople jockey for the next sales management position.
- Some people have difficulty adjusting from being part of the team to leading the team.
- Others have difficulty giving up the activity of the day-to-day sales world to move into the more strategic role of sales management.

The real answer to these potential problems lies with the smart sales organizations who are quick to embrace the idea that they select the best, most qualified people to be sales managers no matter where they can find them. It makes little difference whether they are promoted from within or hired from the outside. The issue is just that simple. The best, most qualified person wins the job.

Different Positions Require Different Attributes

Over several decades, we have learned that there are a set of additional attributes that are uniquely demanded by sales management positions. Obviously, attributes such as systematic thinking and interpersonal skills are critical. We have identified 13 additional attributes that may be far less obvious:

1. Handling stress.
2. Monitoring others.
3. Project and goal focus.
4. Quality orientation.
5. Systems judgment.
6. Understanding motivational needs of others.
7. Conflict and problem resolution.
8. Achieving bottom-line results.
9. Leadership.
10. Opportunity analysis.
11. Planning orientation.
12. Self- and project management.
13. Staffing focus.

These attributes are measured and evaluated in addition to the 23 tightly targeted, job-specific attributes that are discovered through the TriMetrix process as we examine the complex demands of each specific job.

Even a cursory look at these attributes allows you to see the tremendous disparity between the requirements of a sales and sales management role. However, even though there are significant differences, we have identified six attributes as being essential for success in *both* sales and sales management positions:

1. Goal directedness.
2. Handling rejection.
3. Results orientation.
4. Self-starting ability.

5. Handling stress.

6. Self-discipline.

Is it possible for a Super Bowl performer at running back to be a successful coach? Maybe. It totally depends on the player. But to generalize and say that most Super Bowl running backs will (or won't) be a successful coach is erroneous. However, there are a few more issues here. Does every successful running back even want to be a coach in the first place? Does every successful running back know the game well enough to coach others—or was his talent so natural and intuitive as to render him virtually incapable of developing others relative to the skills and techniques so necessary for their peak performance? The examples here between selling and coaching are parallel . . . and obvious. Research also suggests that those who have developed their talents intuitively, like great athletes, are the least effective at teaching those skills to others.

For years, National Football League teams hired former players as assistant coaches, and they would work their way up the coaching ranks to become the league's head coaches. Then, suddenly, there was a huge turnaround. College coaches (most of whom had never set foot on an NFL playing field as players) began to populate the NFL coaching ranks. The result was a much more innovative, creative, exciting, and wide open brand of football.

Virtually all football coaches have played the game. Not all were superstars. In fact, most weren't. To be successful as a sales manager, you need to have logged some time in sales to be able to better understand the dynamics, expectations, pressures, and mechanics of selling. However, like the coach, does the sales manager have to have been a superstar? Probably not. It could be argued that having been a superstar might even be a detriment because an immature superstar might have trouble moving from being the center of attention to the facilitator of others' success. And, like the Super Bowl running back or others with great natural talent, the superstar salesperson may have had such natural talent that he or she finds it difficult to communicate what it takes to be successful or may lack the fundamental attributes that the job requires.

In any case, the hiring and training of sales managers is just as important as is the process for selecting the right salespeople. In fact, hiring and training sales managers is probably more important because of the tremendous influence that this person has in the success or failure of the entire sales team. It is not a responsibility to be taken lightly. Recall that 68 percent of our respondents polled told us they solely promoted from within. That certainly does limit the applicant pool, doesn't it?

What Should Sales Managers Do When They Are in the Job?

There are primarily two functions that sales managers in smart companies perform. First, they establish clear standards and expectations. Second, they provide feedback against those standards and expectations. These two functions form the nucleus for everything else to follow. We discuss the many additional responsibilities later.

Establishing expectations means the creation of standards. And these standards should be much more than just sales objectives. Unfortunately, in too many sales organizations, that single expectation is all there is. How many of this or of that should a salesperson sell? If the salesperson exceeds the expectations for sales volume, all is well. If not, things aren't so good.

In smart companies, however, there are tighter metrics. Samples of these metrics are standards relative to:

- Margin on sales.
- Closing ratios and percentages.

- Customer retention.
- Vertical integration of accounts.
- Compliance with reporting of data.
- Professionalism and image.
- Teamwork.
- Delivery of key job accountabilities.
- Delivery of attributes.
- Delivery of expected behaviors.
- Cost containment.
- Adherence to budget requirements.
- Minimal lead acquisition cost.

Set Expectations

Expectations are all about establishing a level of performance that can be monitored, measured, and evaluated against a standard that must be met. The job of the sales manager should be to establish those standards and ensure compliance with them. This requires systematic, regular evaluation and meaningful feedback against those standards. For some people, the evaluation and feedback process can be uncomfortable, even unsavory when they have to deliver bad news. They must not only deliver the bad news, but also they have to take action on it. And, aren't sales managers supposed to motivate salespeople, not punish them? Isn't punishment demotivating?

Give Feedback

Giving feedback is the corrective side of things. Feedback needs to be honest, sincere, consistent, and as objective as possible. Smart companies do this with a regular appraisal system.

Initially, feedback should be done as often as quarterly, then semiannually. We have encountered sales organizations that have no performance reviews at all. Others give a cursory review related to sales performance only. We have seen others who use the same review format for everyone in the entire organization regardless of the position. As a consequence, the process is badly watered down and viewed as unimportant. Any meaningful review must be geared solely and exclusively to that position (see Chapter 8 for more detail).

Sales Management Is Really a Teaching and Coaching Job

Perhaps the most essential roles that smart companies have their sales managers perform are those of teaching and coaching. I was recently contacted by one of our CEO clients who wanted to schedule a luncheon meeting. He said, "I need to have lunch with you as soon as possible. I've figured this sales thing out and want to tell you about it."

I showed up at 11:45 A.M. and he was already there. As we were hustled to our table, I could see his excitement. Once we sat down, he looked around the restaurant as if to ensure that what he would tell me would not be overheard by anyone. He leaned across the table and whispered to me, "You have to coach them every day." My response? "Is that all?" He responded, "Of course not. You have to *teach* them what to do first. Then go into the field and *coach* them every day."

This may not sound like a big deal. But it is a big, big deal. This CEO's company has increased sales every year for more than 15 years and continues to grow regardless of the economic climate, world affairs, political situations, competitive factors, or anything else its market can throw at it.

Yes, it is just that simple. However, getting sales managers who can teach or coach is not that easy. Getting them to have or make the time, have the interest, or display the inclination to do it is even more difficult. Unfortunately, because of time pressures and daily demands, it becomes easier to be consumed by the immediacies that bring a sense of closure, of feeling important and being needed, and having the reassuring feeling of having saved the day that fuels the short-term thinking of many sales managers.

The real secret to being a smart sales manager in a smart company lies in making teaching and coaching the top priority. It lies in teaching and coaching salespeople to have the confidence and skills to meet the standards that are set and then to give them both positive and corrective feedback against those standards. This then yields a consistently improving sales organization.

Effective sales management and leadership result in a high prospect-to-closing ratio and a well-paid team that is enthusiastic; ineffective sales management can lead to lost sales, internal friction, deteriorating morale, and disorganization.

CHAPTER 4

THE SUPERIOR SELLING CHAPTER REVIEW

- The quality of sales management that a sales team receives ultimately determines the quality of its performance.

- Sales management is an inexact science because of the multiple human variables at play within the complex sales arena.

- Sales managers need a strong understanding of the social sciences to be successful. The job of sales manager is far more than business management. It is the ultimate human capital management business.

- Too many sales organizations tend to undervalue the critical role that the careful selection of sales managers plays in their organizational success.

■ It is an error to automatically promote strong salespeople into sales management positions because of five reasons:

Reason 1: The belief that superior sales skills automatically translate into superior sales management skills.

Reason 2: A reluctance to place someone into the sales management position who has not proven his or her sales mettle to the sales team.

Reason 3: An assumption that unless someone has been the top salesperson, the sales team will not respect or follow that person.

Reason 4: The belief that every salesperson wants to move into sales management.

Reason 5: The contention that industry experience coupled with field sales experience automatically qualifies someone for a sales management position.

■ When a highly successful salesperson is taken from the field and placed into a sales management position, two bad things can occur. First, the organization loses the productivity of a top sales professional. Second, there is often an unwilling or unqualified sales manager in place.

■ The answer to these potential problems lies with smart sales organizations that are quick to embrace the idea that they should select the best, most qualified people to be sales managers—no matter where they can find them. It makes little difference whether they are promoted from within or hired from the outside—the best, most qualified person wins the job.

■ There are 13 specific attributes generally necessary for sales management success:

Attribute 1: Handling stress.

Attribute 2: Monitoring others.

Attribute 3: Project and goal focus.

Attribute 4: Quality orientation.

Attribute 5: Systems judgment.

Attribute 6: Understanding motivational needs of others.

Attribute 7: *Conflict and problem resolution.*

Attribute 8: *Achieving bottom-line results.*

Attribute 9: *Leadership.*

Attribute 10: *Opportunity analysis.*

Attribute 11: *Planning orientation.*

Attribute 12: *Self- and project management.*

Attribute 13: *Staffing focus.*

■ A person does not have to have been a superstar salesperson to be a great sales manager.

■ The two primary functions that sales managers perform are to establish clear standards and expectations and to provide feedback against those standards and expectations.

■ Tight metrics relative to salespeople's achievement of standards need to be developed by sales managers, for example:

Metric 1: *Margin on sales.*

Metric 2: *Closing ratios and percentages.*

Metric 3: *Customer retention.*

Metric 4: *Vertical integration of accounts.*

Metric 5: *Compliance with reporting of data.*

Metric 6: *Professionalism and image.*

Metric 7: *Teamwork.*

Metric 8: *Delivery of key accountabilities.*

Metric 9: *Delivery of attributes.*

Metric 10: *Delivery of expected behaviors.*

Metric 11: *Cost containment.*

Metric 12: *Adherence to budget requirements.*

Metric 13: *Minimal lead acquisition cost.*

■ Sales managers have to be willing to deliver both the good and bad news through feedback and corrective action.

- Performance management and appraisal sessions should be held at least twice per year, and the form or system that is used should be geared seamlessly to the sales position being evaluated.

- Teaching and coaching skills are essential competencies for sales managers to master. In fact, these skills are the top priority for successful sales managers.

- The bottom line: Effective sales management and leadership results in a high prospect-to-closing ratio and a well-paid team that is enthusiastic; ineffective sales management can lead to lost sales, internal friction, deteriorating morale, and disorganization.

Sales Management Process

An Eight-Step Process

To build a great sales team, a meaningful and consistent sales management process must be in place organizationwide. It must be systematic and implemented by systematic people. The process needs to be ongoing and able to be monitored for effectiveness. This process, ideally, should contain the following components:

- Recruitment.
- Selection.
- Establishing expectations.
- Ongoing training.
- Coaching.
- Feedback and course correction.
- Measurable accountability.
- Sustaining momentum.

For this process to be in place and workable, sales managers must have both the responsibility (the obligation to perform) and authority (the right to act) to make all eight of these components happen. Responsibility without authority leads to nothing but frustration. Authority without responsibility can lead to abuse. Both of these situations are wrong. But coupling no responsibility with no authority is the worst thing that can happen to a person. It doesn't take long for everyone in the organization to know that the sales management team is powerless . . . and it doesn't take long for the sales management team to seek employment elsewhere (if they're good) or "quit and stay" (if they're not good enough to be hired elsewhere). This issue is discussed in great depth later.

An In-Depth Look

Let's look at each of the eight steps in the process.

Step 1: Recruitment

Recruitment is the very lifeblood of any sales organization. Sales managers need to be recruiting constantly. Smart companies are looking for great salespeople even when they feel they don't need more salespeople. Your organization needs to be an attractive, desirable place to be. Again, don't limit yourself to those with just industry experience. Attract the very best you can and be known for having a positive, yet demanding, sales environment. That is what great salespeople are looking for, and there are a multitude of ways to recruit great salespeople. As a general rule, the wider the net, the more candidates you attract. Whether it is Internet based, association or organization driven, or a networking process, the key is to be recruiting all the time, even if you don't feel you need people. Your goal? To always be raising the bar and taking it to the point that your salesforce is made up of nothing but great salespeople. To prove that there is always a need for better and better salespeople, I often ask sales executives this simple question: How much market share do you have? I've never heard "all of it." There is always room for more sales, salespeople, and growth.

Step 2: Selection

Always select with great caution. Use multiple interviews and interviewers. Benchmark the position you're looking to fill. Be sure to incorporate some sort of in-depth, valid assessment that measures the full array of capacities that help identify a successful salesperson for your unique, one-of-a-kind sales job. Take your time and don't be tempted to shortcut the process to fill a slot on the roster. That can be a fatal error. Those who are being considered need to know how much and exactly what is expected of them so they can opt out before they are hired. Consider only applicants who meet the exact standards of the job. Don't be tempted into a fast hire. Remember, it is far easier to get into anything than it is to get out of it. Use multiple interviews and interviewers, and make the process rigorous and demanding. Do social screening and take your time.

Step 3: Establishing Expectations

Design a meaningful and in-depth orientation program for new salespeople. Your program needs to enculturate them into the unique environment that defines your organization. New salespeople need to understand the culture as it is defined by the norms, values, and expectations of your company. They need to know the attributes they are expected to master, the values and behaviors that are rewarded (and not rewarded), dress and style, expectations, both the formal and informal structure, etiquette standards, travel standards, reporting structure, paperwork, and/or digital requirements that your unique environment demands. Fail to do this and you set both of you up for failure and frustration.

Step 4: Ongoing Training

The importance of ongoing training is often overlooked and underestimated. Sales managers often believe that if they hire only experienced salespeople, they will come fully prepared to perform. Wrong. Others believe that product knowledge training is enough. Wrong. Some believe that salespeople will learn, study, and eventually master their craft on their own. Also wrong.

The real key to a successful training program is that it must be ongoing. It cannot be an event. Event training is simply not enough. I cannot tell you the number of times that our firm has been called to "come in and train these people at our annual meeting." That is a waste of our time, their money, and everyone's effort.

This is best characterized by a recent experience I had with a well-known financial services organization. I received an e-mail from the vice president of sales asking if I could attend their annual meeting and give them a "dose of sales training." Just as I do with everyone, I responded by saying that I'd recommend that we at least consider a longer term, systematic process. He didn't like my response, thinking I was trying to sell him something. So, instead, he decided to bring in a motivational speaker. I wonder what carryover value that three-hour session had. Did it really change anything on a long-term basis? I doubt it.

Selling skills that must be taught are strongly dependent on each sales situation. For example, complex selling situations require a different approach than do simpler ones. C-level selling is different from calling on lower level buyers, selling through distribution is different from selling direct, and so on. However, as a general rule, the following skills are essential and must be taught to salespeople, no matter what their selling venue may be:

- Positioning.
- Prospecting.
- Precall planning.
- Building and sustaining trust.
- Questioning and qualifying.
- Delivering targeted presentations.
- Selling value.
- Handling objections.
- Application-based selling.
- Finalizing transactions.
- Listening skills.
- Time and territory management.

Step 5: Coaching

Coaching is far different from training. Training imparts ideas, concepts, or strategies in a safe environment. Coaching, on the other hand, means active involvement in the field. It means engaging the prospect while the salesperson is receiving meaningful, valuable direction from the sales manager.

This is another missing link in the life of most salespeople. Far too many receive little or no coaching. Our research reveals it and our experience shows it.

The most common reason we encounter for a breakdown in coaching is a consistent refrain that comes from both large and small organizations alike and from every corner of the world: time—or better yet, a lack of time.

We hear that sales managers have entirely too much to do. Unfortunately, much of it often has little to do with sales management. For example, the sales manager who has to deal with his or her own block of business, has administrative duties to handle, operational tasks to complete, paperwork to process, marketing duties to undertake, ordering to finalize, office politics to juggle, protection of the salesforce from other departments to be done, keeping battling salespeople from each other's throats, a lead management system to track, implementation of a failing CRM system, and so on. And the list could be much longer.

With all of that to do, what suffers? Time in the field. And in the field is where the real coaching has to occur. Athletic coaches cannot coach their teams from their offices. They need to be on the rink, court, diamond, links, or field. Military field officers cannot lead their troops from their bunkers. Sales managers need to be with their salespeople when the salespeople are engaging the customer. There is simply no way around it.

However, coaching means far more than just physically being there. It means having a system or process in which meaningful coaching can occur. Sales organizations need a sales philosophy to coach, a linked and sequential sales process in which the coaching occurs, and a process that enables this coaching experience to be meaningful and substantive. And this process goes all the way back to expectations that are initially set along with the initial installation of this same philosophy or system during the training phase of this process.

Strong sales coaches never miss an opportunity to coach, whether it's in the hallway, between meetings, on the way to a sales call, following a sales call, or at lunch. Strong coaches seek every opportunity to ensure that their salespeople are constantly being reminded of exactly how they can perform better, more effectively, or with better results.

Step 6: Feedback and Course Correction

There is an old saying: "The best way around is straight through." In this context, it means that sales managers must have the courage to provide both good and constructive feedback as quickly and regularly as possible. They also have to see the feedback as being important, must make the time to do it, need to know how to do it, and must make it part of their on-going way of working with their sales team.

We installed a coaching and feedback system with one of our clients over a several-year period. This organization had around 400 salespeople and 60 sales managers. When we started, they had no consistent sales process, training methodology, coaching system, or anything else. They also hadn't hit their sales targets for four to five years in a row.

It took about 18 months to integrate the coaching process for their sales managers, the main part of which was the feed-back and course-correction component. The most difficult part of the process was getting the sales managers to understand two things:

1. Their *real* job was the development of their salespeople.
2. Feedback and course correction were *not* punitive, but developmental.

However, it goes back further than that. We first had to get the senior management of the organization to understand and be 100 percent committed to three things:

1. Ongoing training.
2. Allowing the sales managers the time and latitude to get into the field.
3. Communicating that this process was all about growth and improvement performance, not eliminating people.

If you fail to get senior management on board relative to these three concepts, your entire sales development process will never flourish. It absolutely must be done.

Feedback is essential to the success of anyone, whether it is a quarterly blood test for diabetes or cholesterol, an annual phys-ical for overall health, an occasional step on your scale, a blood pressure check, or any other evaluation for healthful living. The same is true for salespeople.

But the only way to give meaningful feedback is to provide it in real-time ways. You must be in the field, watching salespeople interface with customers, asking them questions and evaluating their answers, observing them interact with customers, and evaluating how they handle customer problems or difficulties. Don't fall prey to the mistaken belief that you can rely on call reports, sales results, or other historical data to use as real-time feedback tools. It just doesn't work like that.

Smart companies also have a method of tracking those activities that they deem most necessary to lead to successful sales. Activities that need to be tracked on a daily basis include:

- Self-generated prospects.
- Earned referrals.
- Contact referrals.
- Face-to-face appointments scheduled.
- Telephone presentations made.
- Face-to-face presentations made.
- Proposals generated.
- Completed sales.

Course correction is the next part of this phase of the formula. *Course correction* simply means giving the salesperson a way to improve or enhance his or her performance. But remember Universal Sales Management Truth 5: "You can't lead where you won't go any more than you are able to teach the things you don't know." If you're not willing to get in the field, this won't happen. And if you don't know exactly what someone needs to do to improve, you have another, more fundamental problem. Unfortunately, so does the salesperson. It's you.

Step 7: Measurable Accountability

This part of the process often proves to be emotionally elusive for many sales organizations because there is a stronger tendency to talk about holding people accountable than there is a willingness to actually do it. Whatever the reason, the results are the same. In the final analysis, there are many people with subpar results, a few with superior results, and a great deal of confusion as to why.

Measurable accountability starts with establishing objectives—easy-to-monitor performance standards that ensure a person is moving toward successful achievement of the predetermined sales objectives that have been established, for example:

- Completion of measurable activities over a period of time (calls, contracts, presentations, proposals, etc.).
- Completion of training programs, activities, or sequences with measurable outcomes that show a level of understanding.
- Demonstrated competencies relative to specific activities (e.g., demonstrated capacity to complete reports, facility with software).
- Sales results with a careful eye toward volume, margin, lead management, accounts penetrated, product mix sold, and so on. Note, however, that sales volume is one of the last things on this list. Although sales volume is important, successful completion of other things ensures that volume will occur.

This all demands much more than showing people videos or DVDs and then hoping they will go sell something. It is the capacity and willingness to measure their level of understanding and knowledge. It is determining the level of commitment they have made to expend the effort required to be successful and then holding them accountable for the actual learning, retention, and demonstrated performance of what they have been expected to master and deliver.

Step 8: Sustaining Momentum

The most difficult, demanding part is the phase of the process that requires a sales manager to be persistent and dogged. This phase requires a sales organization to keep the wheels turning and the energy level consistent. It is the difference between a flash in the pan, short-term burst of success and the legacy that is built through a sustained effort. And not every organization has the fortitude to see it through.

Sustaining momentum requires a repeat of the same process again and again. The problem is that everyone is not built for the long haul. Many people and organizations don't have the dogged determination of a Winston Churchill or a Gandhi. And that is a shame, because dogged and tireless determination is fundamentally what it takes.

Simply repeat the process:

- Recruit—upgrade your sales team consistently. Raise the bar constantly and consistently.
- Select—use the knowledge you garnered from previous mis-hires to avoid the same hiring mistakes.
- Establish expectations—create new, higher, and more demanding standards as your sales organization improves.
- Train—teach advanced skills for longer term salespeople and the basics for new hires.
- Coach—spend time in the field more often and more rigorously to raise the performance levels.
- Measure Accountability—hold salespeople to even higher standards.
- Provide feedback and course-correct—never stop the coaching process.

This process will help to sustain your positive momentum. But it doesn't stop there. You need to start the cycle again. However, it is never that clear, easy, or simple. You will have different salespeople at different phases at different times. Remember, this is a process, not an event. And it is a process that is continuous, evolving, and ever changing. It's not for the weak or faltering. But neither is success because if success were easy, everyone and every organization would be successful.

It's All about Achieving Goals

Sales success is based on ultimately achieving a set of predetermined sales goals or objectives within a prescribed time frame. Smart companies understand that they and their salespeople must jointly develop sales targets that salespeople will be committed to achieving.

Not-so-smart companies do it very differently. These old-school throwbacks have a tendency to tell salespeople what they are supposed to do. They mandate quotas, sales targets, or goals. The result? Salespeople never emotionally buy into assigned targets, there is no psychological ownership of them, and it becomes difficult to ensure commitment to those activities that will eventually lead to their successful accomplishment.

On the other hand, smart companies ensure that salespeople are legitimately excited, buy into, and are totally committed to achieving those things the salespeople themselves have committed to do.

There are five potential landmines that must be avoided at all costs:

1. Don't give someone an automatic increase in sales goals based on his or her previous year's performance.
2. Don't give across-the-board sales increases for the entire sales team.

3. Don't assign quotas without a salesperson's input.

4. Don't believe that someone will perform optimally if something is not his or her idea—including a sales quota.

5. Never fail to provide regular, consistent, short-term feedback relative to long-term sales results.

To make this process work, smart sales leaders meet with their sales teams significantly before the end of a calendar or fiscal year, review performance, and jointly discuss what the next year's performance should look like with each salesperson. They are careful not to let salespeople's emotions go unchecked to the point that they commit themselves to unattainable goals. However, they are also careful to ensure that salespeople stretch themselves toward the successful achievement of positive sales targets.

Once this is done, ongoing feedback must be provided against a public set of sales targets that salespeople have committed themselves to achieving. Information that is shared, posted, and made public virtually guarantees that a person will do all in his or her power to meet or exceed targets. That is the magic of the process. Great salespeople will work day and night to meet or exceed what they have committed publicly to doing.

There is one word of caution here. Success is dependent on having the right people in the jobs in the first place. It's amazing, isn't it? Everything always goes back to having the right people—it's first, foremost, and always the key to any organization's sales success. And it always will be.

CHAPTER 5

THE SUPERIOR SELLING CHAPTER REVIEW

■ To build a great sales team, a strong sales management process must be in place.

■ Responsibility without authority leads to nothing but frustration. Authority without responsibility can lead to abuse.

■ Recruitment is the very lifeblood of any sales organization.

■ Always select with great caution. Use multiple interviews and interviewers. Benchmark the position you're looking to fill. Then be sure to incorporate in-depth, valid assessment tools that measure the full array of capacities that help to identify a successful salesperson for your unique job.

■ Design a meaningful, in-depth orientation program for new salespeople. Your program needs to enculturate them into the unique environment that defines your organization.

■ The real key to a successful training program is that it must be ongoing.

■ As a general rule, the following skills are essential and must be taught to salespeople, no matter what their selling venue may be:

Skill 1: Positioning.

Skill 2: Prospecting.

Skill 3: Precall planning.

Skill 4: Building and sustaining trust.

Skill 5: Questioning and qualifying.

Skill 6: Delivering targeted presentations.

Skill 7: Selling value.

Skill 8: Handling objections.

Skill 9: Application-based selling.

Skill 10: Finalizing transactions.

Skill 11: Listening skills.

Skill 12: Time and territory management.

■ Coaching is far different from training. Training imparts ideas, concepts, or strategies in a safe environment. Coaching, on the other hand, means active involvement in the field.

- Sales managers must have the courage to provide both good and constructive feedback as quickly and regularly as possible.

- Measurable accountability often proves to be elusive for many sales organizations because there is a stronger tendency to talk about holding people accountable than there is a willingness to actually do it.

- Sustaining momentum is the most difficult, demanding component of the sales management process. This is the phase of the process that requires a sales manager to be persistent and dogged.

- Sales success is based on ultimately achieving a set of predetermined sales goals or objectives within a prescribed time frame.

- To get salespeople excited about achieving sales targets, you must avoid the following at all costs:

  1. Don't give someone an automatic increase in sales goals based solely on previous year's performance.

  2. Don't give across-the-board sales increases for the entire sales team.

  3. Don't assign quotas without a salesperson's input.

  4. Don't ever believe that someone will perform optionally if something is not his or her idea—including a sales quota.

  5. Never fail to provide regular, short-term feedback relative to long-term sales results.

6

Achieving Total Selling Mastery

The Power of the Right
Orientation Program

When most people hear the term *orientation*, they think about programs preparing freshmen for entry into college. Research in higher education indicates that the quality of those orientation programs, in large measure, determines the long-term retention of students over a four-year period. Bottom line? Strong orientation programs aid in retention anywhere, including in smart selling companies.

The military spends a big chunk of time preparing new recruits for their military experience as well. Everything they do is designed for the very same reason: to retain the recruits they have worked hard to convert from applicants to solid military personnel, who, if qualified, will consider a long-term military career.

What about sales organizations? Orientation programs are spotty, at best. Their traditional view toward this concept has gone from a visit to the benefits or human resources department to the "here's your desk" strategy for new salespeople. Many sales organizations, unfortunately, offer no type of formal orientation program of any significant, long-term value to salespeople. The larger the organization, the more likely there is to be some form of orientation. The smaller, the more likely there will be a minimal effort in this direction.

Some argue that they hire only experienced salespeople (we've seen the fallacy of that argument), others claim that they do a thorough enough job, while others are honest enough to say that they just don't know what to do.

There are many things about a new employer and a new job that recently hired salespeople need to know as they enter into their new environment. This is true no matter what their level of experience in sales or whatever they have sold, even if they have sold a similar product, they have a background in the industry, or they are moving from another department into a sales role.

What fundamentally needs to be learned can be broken into three categories as shown in Figure 6.1.

Three Key Areas of Knowledge

Information imparted to salespeople in this initial phase of their orientation process will prove to be critical to their long-term

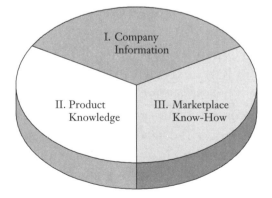

FIGURE 6.1   **Company, Product, Marketplace Circle**

success. It provides them a solid grounding into the essential things that they must not only learn, but eventually master. Without information eventually being mastered in the following three key areas, a salesperson will always be operating from a strategic disadvantage:

1. *Company information* is far more than just the history of the organization. Instead, it deals with its philosophy, mission, vision, standards, policies, procedures, paperwork, pay plan, benefits, systems, and processes. But it is more than that. It reveals the very culture of the organization to the new salesperson—the norms, values, and expectations that together make the organization what it is and its richness, uniqueness, and philosophy.

2. *Product knowledge* is part of that culture. Essential information includes data, parts codes, product numbers, background, application and features, benefits, advantages, and solutions that the product or service uniquely provides to customers. What problems does it solve? How is it designed? How does it compare to the competition? What are the most glaring weaknesses of the product or service? What questions will the salesperson be asked most often? What should the answers be?

3. *Marketplace know-how* is not only the positioning of the salesperson's company and products relative to others, but also how it relates to that competition, competitor's customers, competitive factors it faces, market trends that are occurring, industry or trade publications to be read, organizations to be joined, associations to be a part of, networking opportunities to seek, unique features of the marketplace relative to time frames, events, macrotrends, national and international events, and everything that forms the landscape of the marketplace.

Simply imparting this knowledge is not enough. Giving salespeople sufficient time to understand, assimilate, and apply the information is essential. As we discuss later in the chapter, the secret here is one essential thing: Total learning mastery.

Are You Being Held Hostage?

Unfortunately, some sales organizations have their most essential knowledge bottled up inside experienced salespeople's heads. It has never been catalogued, archived, or put into any usable format for transfer of the information to newly hired salespeople.

One dysfunctional manifestation of this is a reluctance or refusal to hire new salespeople simply because there is no way to transfer the knowledge. A more alarming result is resorting to hiring only people with experience in the market so that less knowledge has to be transferred. The most common solution, having the experienced salesperson impart the knowledge to the new person on a one-on-one basis, is, unfortunately, the most flawed approach of all. Evidence shows that self-taught experts are often the most ineffective at teaching others. Remember the NFL example?

In most organizations, the knowledge that resides in the heads of experienced people is lost when they are transferred to another division, leave, or retire. We have developed a method to solve this problem in a unique way. However, smart companies can do the same thing themselves. They must strategically and carefully interview experienced salespeople to learn what is "in their heads." They must then archive the most valuable information and organize it into a self-directed learning system for new salespeople. All of it must be organized and carefully coordinated for maximum learning potential. You need to be able to retrieve decades of invaluable experience, knowledge, and wisdom and make it available for instant learning, retention, and use for new or less experienced salespeople. Our process, which is software driven, guarantees 80 percent learning mastery of the material. However, smart companies, if they are willing to invest the time, can do the same thing on their own.

That raises another interesting question: Just what is mastery? I often ask a roomful of sales executives this question: "What do you have a superior level of mastery at doing?" Some examples have been:

- Bass fishing.
- Marketing.
- Racing my boat.
- Understanding software.
- Selling.
- Playing chess.
- Riding my motorcycle.
- Repairing equipment.
- Driving my car.

Mastery means that people are so well drilled and in control of every facet of what it is they are doing that they respond intuitively. They have such an in-depth, internal, and complete understanding of what they do that they don't even need to think about the basics behind doing it. How about driving your car? Do you have to stop and think about everything you do? Insert key, turn key, place in drive, keep foot on brake, check rearview mirrors, and so on? No, you just do it.

Salespeople need to have just as strong a level of mastery over as much company, product, marketplace, and sales information as fast as they possibly can to be competitive in today's fast-paced, demanding market. If you fail to bring them up to speed as quickly as possible, you, they, and your entire organization are vulnerable. If you fail to begin archiving and organizing this information now for new generations of salespeople, you are in trouble there, too. If you are hesitant or downright afraid to hire new people, your organization will eventually die. Look at your salesforce. If you see years and years of experience, be concerned. Perhaps you need to consider ways to capture what they do and how they do it before it's too late. Consider yourself warned. For more than 25 years, I have seen organizations not face this reality and live to regret it.

I once asked a sales executive about this very issue, and she assured me that they were doing a great job of categorizing and organizing the critical sales knowledge in her organization. However, my second question stopped her cold in her tracks: "How do you know that the information you are archiving and downloading is mastered and then used in the field by new salespeople?" She had one answer: "We don't."

The real name of the game is learning mastery. And total mastery occurs only when a salesperson has complete control over every facet of product knowledge, company, organizational, marketplace, and sales know-how as quickly and as thoroughly and confidently as possible. Presenting information to people is one thing. Knowing that they have learned it is quite another. One definition of *self-confidence* is "knowing that you know." Perhaps another is "mastery."

Smart companies not only hire smart salespeople, but also equip them with the necessary sales and personal skills to be successful. Although these are skills separate from mastery of knowledge related to product, service, and marketplace factors, they do include essential skills that salespeople must master to be able to perform successfully.

As discussed in the previous chapter, sales skills that salespeople must master range from positioning and prospecting to precall planning, territory management, face-to-face selling, account management, and a host of specific skill sets related to the profession of sales and to each sales organization and each sales position's unique demands.

However, just like sales management skills, there are a host of selling principles that should serve as the infrastructure around which any sales approach can be crafted. This chapter explains the 12 most essential selling principles that successful sales organizations ensure their salespeople understand.

Our research of sales organizations is very telling about the transfer of this knowledge, what it is exactly, and how it is best accomplished. We discovered that 73 percent of the organizations surveyed provide some form of formal sales training for their salespeople. However, only 50 percent provide regular in-the-field coaching by a sales manager. That means there is a disaster of monumental proportions waiting to happen. In fact, it probably already has. They just don't know it yet.

The problem? Selling skills can be initially taught, but to be mastered, they must be coached, reinforced, and constantly upgraded in the field. In the absence of a solid foundation of principles that can be subsequently enhanced and improved, there will be little or no improvement or sustained acceleration from the novice to the mastery level. As we have mentioned repeatedly, however, a failure to reinforce even the best principles will cause any effort to fail.

The 12 Most Universal Sales Truths

Here are the 12 most universal sales truths that we have seen work in any sales environment, selling any product or service, anywhere to anybody.

Universal Sales Truth 1: Prospects Pay Attention to Someone Who They Believe Has Something Important to Say to Them

This principle is all about how salespeople are viewed by prospects relative to the knowledge and perspective that they bring to the marketplace. However, it is far more than that. It is also about how they position themselves as professionals who deliver solutions, bring expertise, and offer value to every prospect.

Salespeople who still naively position themselves solely as sales-people have a great deal of difficulty understanding this principle because salespeople, as a group, are stereotypically viewed with less than universal admiration. In addition, today's prospects are looking for more than what a "sales rep" can deliver.

When you are positioned as an industry expert, author, business expert, advocate, or advisor, the view changes 180 degrees. Being viewed as a well-positioned businessperson is what it's all about. The result is greater receptivity in the marketplace, wider and freer access to decision makers at higher levels, and a stronger series of sales opportunities based far more on pulling desirable prospects to them than pushing themselves onto unsuspecting prospects.

Sales managers and executives need to establish a climate and methodology for salespeople to implement this process. They also, however, must provide salespeople with the tools and capacity to position themselves in the most effective way. The days of cold-calling, phone canvassing, and finding prospects who are willing to talk to a poorly positioned salesperson have come and gone, at least for great salespeople and the smart companies they represent.

Universal Sales Truth 2: The Secret to Selling Is to Be in Front of Qualified Prospects When They Are Ready to Buy, Not When You Need to Make a Sale

Let there be little doubt, when and whether prospects will decide to buy anything has far more to do with *their* time schedule than the time schedule of *any* salesperson. By the same token, the key to selling anything to anybody is all about having a sufficient supply of qualified prospects and then being the one who is there when they are ready to make a purchase decision.

In today's digital-driven society, it is easy to stay in touch with prospects. But two words of caution here. First, don't become so obsessed with some sort of digital contact management system that it consumes most of the salesperson's day just to manage it. Keep it simple. Second, be sure never to abandon old-fashioned salesmanship even though the twenty-first century is so digitally dependent. Face-to-face selling still works. Use twenty-first century tools to keep salespeople in front of prospects, but don't forget the basics. Great headlines still work (e.g., "Free Special Report . . . Offered for the Second and Last Time"), as do direct response methods ("Click on this link to receive this report") and urgency ("Offer expires on June 30").

Universal Sales Truth 3: Listen People into Buying instead of Talking Your Way Out of the Sale

I recently tried to help a salesperson who was out of a job. He didn't want to relocate, so I contacted the CEO of a local firm to see if I could help. I didn't know that the two had met through a previous business relationship and simply asked the CEO if he knew this person, hoping that he might know of a potential job opening somewhere in the local area.

The CEO's answer: "Yes. I know him. Unfortunately, I wouldn't hire him on a bet . . . and no one else should, either. In fact, you ought to know more about this guy before you try to be the Good Samaritan."

I was taken aback. He went on, "This guy won't shut up. He sells his product and then buys it back. Until he learns to keep his mouth shut, he'll never make a decent living as a salesperson."

Being inquisitive, I looked further into the salesperson's background. Obviously, I should have done it sooner and should have known better. I learned that he had experienced difficulty in every sales job he'd ever had because of the same problem. He had a glittering personality (remember the fallacy of that argument from a previous chapter?), but he simply could not or would not listen. He believed that sales was all about telling, presenting, and verbalizing. He was wrong. It is all about asking questions, recording the answers, accurately listening, and allowing prospects to tell you exactly what, how, when, why, and under what conditions they will buy.

I told the salesperson about his problem and now, perhaps, he is at least aware of it as he, unfortunately, continues to go from job to job. He simply can't, or won't, develop mastery over the secret of listening someone into a sale instead of talking his way out of one.

Universal Sales Truth 4: To a Prospect, Any Price Is Too High until He or She Understands the Value of Your Product or Service

Of all of the twentieth-century concepts that have carryover value to this century, value-added selling is the one that can have the greatest long-term impact. However, there is a fundamental precursor to it that is often overlooked.

To deliver value to a prospect, salespeople have to first understand what the prospect perceives as value. Although this is essential, it is so fundamental that it is often totally disregarded. It is still true that one person's trash is another person's treasure.

This concept has a direct relationship to price. If you have salespeople who prematurely quote price, they will never have a chance to create value for their offering. The reason? Overcoming the traumatic, shocking impact that presenting *any* price too early in the process has had on the prospect.

Here is the process. Smart salespeople first determine what the prospect perceives as value and then present their product or service strictly in terms that communicate what that value means to that specific prospect. They hold off any discussion of price until they have created a sense of value in the mind of the buyer. They also know how to present price, when to do so, and exactly how to position their organization's value proposition in the most appropriate way to each prospect because each prospect's perception of value could, be very, very different.

Universal Sales Truth 5: The Fatal Flaw in Selling Occurs When Salespeople Are so Focused on What They Want to Happen That They Lose Sight of What the Prospect Wants to Happen

This truth is all about focus, philosophy, and direction. It all starts at the top with management and the fundamental message it sends to salespeople throughout the entire organization. Smart companies communicate the very simple premise that they are in business to help their customers get what they want, satisfy needs, solve problems, improve processes, enhance performance, reduce costs, or whatever else may be their customer's intention.

However, they also know that not every prospect or customer is a good one—that not all are created equal. They know that sales is about margin and not just volume. Not everyone is a legitimate prospect, which means simply that the secret to selling is prospecting—not selling. If what you or your organization want is totally opposite of what your prospects want, perhaps they are simply the wrong prospects for you.

The growth of this fatal flaw can be sped up with contests designed to reduce inventories of old product, incentives that drive salespeople to sell things that don't really enhance a customer's application of the products or services they buy, and, frankly, that force salespeople to do things that fly in the face of this principle.

As a sales executive or leader, your goal should be to do all in your power to ensure that salespeople understand, apply, and implement this principle to enhance their sales career and your organization's reach in the marketplace.

Universal Sales Truth 6: Always Tailor Your Presentation to the Prospect's Needs and Wants, Not to Yours

This is another principle that sounds disarmingly fundamental and basic. However, it is so elemental that it, too, is often overlooked. The classic 25-slide digital presentation with a standard set of materials falls on deaf ears in today's competitive marketplace. Inflexible presentations have done nothing more than replace the old-school, outdated flipchart presentations of the twentieth century that, too, were used clumsily. They have, in fact, become nothing more than electronic flipcharts.

What is really required is the capacity to understand how a prospect wants to see your product or service and present it in exactly that way. For example, one prospect may want to see your product or service solve his problem as "ABC," the next may want to see her problems solved in "CBA" format, the next as "BAC," and the very next as "XYZ."

This requires total mastery of product knowledge, extensive precall planning and questioning, and a presentation that can be tailored, customized, altered, modified, or totally overhauled instantly to reflect the findings that salesperson has uncovered.

The twentieth-century beliefs that were exposed in Chapter 1 have eventually become outdated myths that have been replaced with true twenty-first century, smart selling skills. Canned sales presentations are insulting to today's educated and alert customers, many of whom are highly skilled, demanding buyers.

Universal Sales Truth 7: The Jump from Character (What You Are) to Reputation (What People Think You Are) Is Much Smaller than Most Salespeople Would Like to Believe

Today's markets are more crowded than ever and promise to be that way as far into the future that the mind can conceive. It just won't get any easier any time soon. A salesperson's reputation in the marketplace is one more thing that must be jealously guarded and used as a tool instead of a potential weapon to be used by your competitors against them.

For sales managers, that means a constant vigil to hire only people with character—to mold a sales team built on strong ethics, follow-through, and an uncompromising commitment to promise much to your customers and deliver even more.

It also means that sales leaders and executives must exhibit the highest levels of integrity and character themselves. They need to know that salespeople will follow their leaders in high standards of personal characteristics or low ones. History about corporate scandal and misdeeds points that out very clearly.

Smart companies, smart sales leaders, and smart salespeople know that in tight, crowded markets, a solid reputation can be a powerful prospecting, marketing, and selling tool. A poor one can be devastating. Character is still important.

We have seen situation after situation where sales managers hire someone prematurely, without a proper background check, and the results have been disastrous. Doesn't it make sense to know someone's driving record if he or she is driving a company vehicle? One of our background checks revealed a five-page criminal arrest sheet on a client's potential hiree. In other cases, educational or employment credentials were misrepresented. Remember, however, that you must have candidates' approval to conduct the check, and their refusal to allow that check should tell you something, shouldn't it?

Universal Sales Truth 8: Never Violate the Formal Structure of an Organization . . . but Master an Understanding of the Informal

This truth has many ramifications for the organization that wants to have its salespeople selling smart. Many salespeople enter accounts at a level that doesn't match the level of decision making required to make the purchase decision for their product or service. For example, they may enter at very low levels and be dealing with someone who may merely influence a decision, may not want to change the status quo, or has far too little power. They could be selling a product or service that demands an initiative of a larger, more strategic nature. It could involve far-reaching decisions such as totally changing suppliers or initiating a whole new business direction. However, salespeople simply see that they are merely selling a product or service when, in fact, what they are selling could require a whole new inventory management system, an overhauled billing process, a different distribution method, a radical departure from an existing philosophy of business for the prospect, or even more.

The problem? Once salespeople enter too low, it is disastrously difficult to reenter at a higher level. They then have to rely on the person with whom they have been working to get them to that higher level, which is sometimes tough, if not impossible. Lower level prospects often insist on seeing higher levels themselves (and remember, they don't sell your products for a living), stonewall your efforts, or don't want to further your cause for whatever reason.

The fundamental difficulty is that you cannot violate the formal structure of any organization. The formal structure is how the organization is built. It's how the boxes and lines are connected—who reports to whom. But most organizations rarely function totally through any formal structure. They operate through the informal—by whom influences whom most. The formula is to enter as high as you can in the organization and then learn how the informal influence structure works. Most salespeople don't do that. Great salespeople do.

Universal Sales Truth 9: If You Don't Close Sales, You Won't Make a Living as a Salesperson

At first glance, this truth may appear to fly in the face of a twentieth-century myth that was exploded in the first chapter. However, it really doesn't. Making sales is what salespeople do. In reality, it is one of the few professions where there is a real finish line. A salesperson makes the sale or not. It is just that simple. Getting to the finish line is still the key. And in the competitive sales world that promises to continue, the salesperson who has a better, more effective process will get there more often, more successfully, and with a greater margin of victory.

The greatest salespeople develop strong relationships with those customers who want relationships, deliver effective solutions to those customers who are seeking solutions, deliver greater value to those customers who seek value, and offer a speedy transaction to those who seek a quick solution.

Sales is still about making sales. Surgery is still about restoring health and the military is still about securing the peace. But sales is on the prospect's terms.

Therefore, the method by which the sale is made must be totally customer centric. The strategies that are being employed have certainly changed over the years and will continue to change. But the end result—a satisfied customer who is happy to pay your asking price—is still the same.

The greatest salespeople have a method to ensure that this occurs. And the smartest sales organizations are the ones that facilitate the process with proper selection, orientation, training, coaching, products, or services that offer correct pricing, meaningful customer service, on-time delivery, and all of the things that facilitate this end result.

Universal Sales Truth 10: Your Customer Will Never Believe in the Value of Your Product or Service Any More Strongly Than You Do

In many ways, sales is all about belief. It's about belief in yourself and your organization, the efficacy of the product, and believing your product or service is a true value that delivers the promised end result.

For salespeople, it is critical that they totally, 100 percent believe that the product or service they sell is exactly what they say it is and that it will perform exactly the way they say it will.

Our research yields some interesting findings along these lines. We have established that rejection is not as big an issue as some would believe it is for salespeople. However, one of the corollaries to that is the role that embarrassment plays. The real issue is that salespeople don't want to be embarrassed in front of a customer or prospect. It's not the rejection that is the issue. It's the embarrassment. We talk more about this later when we deal with new product releases.

What does that mean for smart companies? They ensure that the products or services they sell exceed the standards they promise to their customers. They spend a great deal of time proving, not to the customer, but to their salespeople, that the things they commit to are exceeded—whether it's the weight tolerance of a piece of heavy equipment, terms of an extended warranty, capacity for a digital product, or a billing procedure. It makes no difference what it is. Salespeople must believe in the value and validity of what it is that they sell.

The downside is what happens to a sales team that is selling something that they don't believe in. The result is a lack of 100 percent, emotional commitment to go to the wall for a product, organization, and team. They just won't sell with the conviction needed to be a great sales team. Your prospects and customers will sense this lack of commitment, too. The result will be exactly what you think it will be—sliding sales and reduced margins.

What does that mean to sales executives and leaders? That their internal customers must be shown and convinced that they are selling a product or service that is even more credible, valuable, and powerful than they could ever expect their prospects or customers to believe and their customers would be foolish not to buy it at any price. Smart organizations have internal campaigns to build belief in themselves and their products on the part of the sales team.

Part of the reason for this problem is that salespeople hear the bad news about product failures, delivery glitches, billing problems, and all the rest before anyone else. They hear it first and fast. Once a lack of belief sets in, it is extremely difficult to eradicate it. Here's the best hint: Use your sales team as the first line of information about problems. Then fix the problems fast. You will have then built a loyal, committed team that will act fast to avoid further embarrassment. The organization will have a better product offering, and the sales team will sell with greater belief. Everyone wins. That is how to be a smart company.

Universal Sales Truth 11: The Better Job You Do of Finding Qualified Prospects, the Higher Your Closing Average Will Be

This is another disarmingly simple truth that has many ramifications. For example, sales organizations that aren't smart mandate that their salespeople:

- Make 50 contacts by phone daily.
- Hit the streets and cold call on no fewer than 30 businesses daily.
- Fill out every form, every time, 100 percent correctly.
- Enter all the necessary data for the marketing department's research effort.

Great salespeople are in front of more qualified people more often. They are not busy doing all the wrong things. A twentieth-century argument says: "You have to make the 50 contacts to find the few qualified ones in the 50." There are scores of intelligent, less demeaning, more exciting ways to identify these qualified prospects with the technology and digital tools that are available today. Smart sales organizations use those tools. Whether it is an electronic newsletter, Internet marketing with a carefully designed web site to build lead generation, or digital intelligence to track interested prospects, there is a full array of simple-to-use tools that are exploding daily.

We have used a wonderful tool that allows us to place an attractive banner on every e-mail we send. The banner can be changed instantly to reflect what we are promoting at that time. For example, "Click here to learn about how you can get an upgrade package at a one-time deep discount." We then have prospects go to a specific web page that allows them to learn more automatically. The system even contacts the appropriate salesperson, who automatically sends prospects an e-mail with one click. The salesperson can then respond to prospects by phone.

The list of these new digital prospecting tools is endless. Smart sales organizations ensure that their salespeople invest most of their time either getting or being in front of qualified prospects. When they do, they close more sales.

Universal Sales Truth 12: Never Make a Claim You Can't Back up with Facts

Prospects expect salespeople to make claims for their product or service. They are impressed, however, when other people do. They are even more impressed when they experience it themselves.

All of these proof sources are based on a simple premise: Claims salespeople make are true. The smartest sales organizations work hard to gather testimonials and research done by third parties to corroborate their claims. They work hard to get other sources to verify that the things they say about their products or services are true.

We have one client with more than 400 salespeople. These salespeople are rewarded when they gather a certain number of letters from happy, satisfied customers. The letters are posted by customer type on the company intranet for easy access by all salespeople nationwide. Each week, new ones are posted so that other salespeople across the country can easily access them. It is not unusual for a salesperson to print 8 to 10 new letters a week for use with their prospects.

Does everyone win in this scenario? This organization sells nationally with salespeople never competing for the same geographical business. However, if in your scenario any crossover could happen, simply come up with a different method. This organization has the potential to post hundreds of letters a week. How about yours?

The same could be done with articles, third-party research, and so on. But the real issue is (1) seeing it as possible, (2) seeing it as important, and then (3) doing it.

All of these Universal Sales Truths are valid. They have stood the test of time. However, they are nothing more than intellectual abstractions unless you can apply them in the field.

Sales is an interesting endeavor. There is so much bad sales information available that, somehow, it gets used more easily than the valuable, meaningful information does. Perhaps the reason is that the bad information is easier to use (provocative questions, etc.) than the good (never make a claim you can't back up with facts). The best practices require more work, coaching, reinforcement, and accountability. And herein lies the challenge.

Smart selling companies provide ongoing coaching. And coaching means reinforcement and accountability. It means time in the field to ensure that the principles that are taught are being adhered to and followed. That is accountability.

A word here about coaching. Smart athletic coaches work hard to ensure that players adhere to the fundamental principles of the game that guarantee success. Examples of fundamental principles from my former world of college football are:

- Keep your shoulders square to the line of scrimmage (defensive line).
- Keep your outside arm free (linebacker).
- Stay as wide as the widest and as deep as the deepest (safety).

In sales, fundamental principles of coaching include:

- People pay attention to people they perceive as having something important to say to them (Universal Sales Truth 1).
- The secret to selling is to be in front of qualified prospects when they are ready to buy, not when you need to make a sale (Universal Sales Truth 2).
- Listen people into buying instead of talking your way out of the sale (Universal Sales Truth 3).

Here's the key to strong coaching: Smart coaches spend as much time telling salespeople *why* to do something as they spend telling them *how* to do it. Salespeople then learn how to do things by practice and repetition that is monitored and observed in the field.

In the final analysis, knowing why to do something is just as essential as knowing how to do it. If you have hired the right people, they will implicitly have the capacity to "do." You then need to give them the coaching that directs them to apply their natural talents in the way you want them to do it.

Remember that smart companies provide a strong orientation to their culture, train people vigorously and aggressively to do the right things, and then provide ongoing coaching to ensure they do them correctly. Coaching is based on the "why" just as much as it is based on the "how." Skills are then monitored with feedback and course correction.

Your goal? To have a great sales team that has total mastery over all they need to know: mastery of product knowledge, your organization's key initiatives, beliefs and philosophy, the marketplace, and how to sell with great belief and value. That's how smart companies sell.

CHAPTER 6
THE SUPERIOR SELLING CHAPTER REVIEW

- Recently hired salespeople need at least a fundamental knowledge about their new employer and job as they enter into their new environment:

  Company information.

  Product knowledge.

  Marketplace know-how.

- In most organizations, the knowledge that resides in the heads of experienced people is lost when they are transferred to another division, leave, or retire.

- *Mastery* means a person is so well drilled and in control of every facet of the task that he or she responds intuitively.

- Salespeople need to have as strong a level of mastery over as much information as fast as possible to be competitive in today's fast-paced, demanding market.

- Total mastery occurs only when a salesperson has complete control over every facet of product knowledge, company, organizational, and marketplace know-how as quickly, thoroughly, and confidently as possible.

- Smart companies not only hire potentially great salespeople, but also equip them with the necessary sales and personal skills to be successful.

- Selling skills can be initially taught, but to be mastered, they must be coached, reinforced, and constantly upgraded in the field.

- The 12 Universal Sales Truths that we have seen work in any sales environment, selling any product or service anywhere, are:

  Truth 1: Prospects pay attention to someone who they believe has something important to say to them.

  Truth 2: The secret to selling is to be in front of qualified prospects when they are ready to buy, not when you need to make a sale.

  Truth 3: Listen people into buying instead of talking your way out of the sale.

  Truth 4: To a prospect, any price is too high until he or she understands the value of your product or service.

  Truth 5: The fatal flaw in selling occurs when salespeople are so focused on what they want to happen that they lose sight of what the prospect wants to happen.

  Truth 6: Always tailor your presentation to the prospect's needs and wants, not to yours.

  Truth 7: The jump from character (what you are) to reputation (what people think you are) is much smaller than most salespeople would like to believe.

  Truth 8: Never violate the formal structure of an organization . . . but master an understanding of the informal.

  Truth 9: If you don't close sales, you won't make a living as a salesperson.

  Truth 10: Your customer will never believe in the value of your product or service any more strongly than you do.

Truth 11: *The better job you do of finding qualified prospects, the higher your closing average will be.*

Truth 12: *Never make a claim you can't back up with facts.*

■ Smart selling companies provide ongoing coaching. Coaching means reinforcement and accountability.

■ Smart coaches spend as much time telling salespeople *why* to do something as they spend telling them *how* to do it.

■ In the final analysis, knowing why to do something is just as essential as knowing how to do it.

7

Sales Culture

Do You Have a True Sales Culture?

Every year our telephone rings many times and the person at the other end, in a panicked voice, asks if we can help them establish or enhance the "sales culture" in their organization.

These calls come from many different organizations. Some are financial institutions trying to figure out how to transform themselves so they can get more competitive, recently deregulated utilities wanting to learn how to compete, or service providers finally realizing that even their in-demand, badly needed services need to be differentiated in the marketplace because of intensified competition. However, a disappointingly large number come from traditional, hard-core sales organizations that have realized they have a serious culture problem (more about this last group of all-too-desperate people later).

The plight of some of these callers is understandable given the circumstances surrounding the first three types of organizations. However, far more perplexing are those organizations that have been legitimately selling for a long time, yet suddenly discover that their sales team is either underperforming, taken for granted, being badly underutilized, being abused, or simply being seen as a necessary evil by other departments in the organization. Yes, they have a sales culture, just not a healthy one. It's one that needs to be fixed and overhauled to survive in the twenty-first century.

In most cases, when we ask sales executives from traditional sales organizations how their salesforce is perceived by internal constituencies, their answers are, "highly professional," "well respected," or even "everyone knows that sales drives the engine."

However, as we begin to dig deeper into the organization, we generally discover that there is a much different picture. It is not uncommon to hear comments from nonsalespeople describe the sales department as:

- Prima donnas.
- Overpromising and underdelivering.
- Promising things we can't deliver at all.
- Obnoxious gladhanders.
- Don't even know the products.
- Messing up our systems.
- Not conforming to company policies.
- Always filling out paperwork incorrectly.
- Disorganized and undisciplined.
- Giving product away.
- Getting in the way.

These are not the types of comments that breed a sense of respect and appreciation for salespeople across the enterprise.

How to Establish a Sales Culture

Based on years of observation across a broad number of companies, certain factors should be present or developed for a solid sales culture to flourish to any level of significance in the organization. First, an organization should decide exactly how it wants to define itself in the broadest sense. There are myriad reasons why an organization might choose to define itself in any certain way: for example, brand, marketplace demands, customer base, competitors, history, expertise, competencies, and infrastructure. This is a very big job that is far beyond our scope here. However, as a general rule, organizations can be defined as having a primary orientation toward:

- Marketing.
- Sales.
- Distribution.
- Service.
- Operations.
- Manufacturing.
- Administration.
- Research and development.
- Engineering.
- Hospitality.

Many organizations really don't know what they are and, as a result, have a climate made up of competing cultures where different departments are battling for control or favor. Each one is hoping to eventually win the day and emerge as the eventual winner, the one that will define the culture. However, regardless of how you should choose to define yourself primarily as a company, at a minimum, a vibrant and respected sales subculture should exist *somewhere* in the organization.

In addition, for salespeople to have even a chance for a positive coexistence, the following must be in place:

1. The sales department must be or have the potential to be profitable.
2. The enterprise must realize and believe that it could not stand solely on its own without a proactive sales effort.
3. The sales department must be championed by a well-placed set of internal constituencies that support the sales effort without equivocation.
4. The sales department must be well managed by respected managers and have performance standards that exceed even the most demanding standards of other departments.
5. Members of the sales department must interface with other departments favorably.
6. The sales department must bring collateral value to the enterprise.
7. The members of the sales department must mesh culturally with enterprisewide standards of performance, decorum, and behavior.
8. The sales department must be made up of competent, capable, high-performance-oriented people.

Let's examine each of these in detail. As we do this, you may want to make a mental note of how your sales team meets each of the standards and what needs to be done to improve deficient areas.

1. The Sales Department Must Be or Have the Potential to Be Profitable

As basic as this may sound, if there are other means by which revenue is being generated that are profitable and productive and the sales team is neither of these, there is a problem. For example, if Internet marketing, direct mail, catalogs, distributors, advertising, or other means of business generation are outdistancing the salesforce's contribution at less cost, the very value of the sales team should be evaluated. However, even if these other means are not in place and the sales team is still not profitable, it is certainly worth considering the replacement of an expensive and nonproducing entity with one that might prove to be more effective and far less expensive to maintain.

On the other hand, if the sales team is able to deliver high-margin, profitable sales and does so consistently while expanding the market and successfully sustaining existing accounts, a different scenario unfolds. It is impossible to justify anything for very long if a business case cannot be made for its existence. The single, most essential thing that must be present for building or sustaining a sales culture is that the salesforce be, or can be, the centerpiece for generating profitable sales. If you remove that potential, you have a case for eliminating a sales team altogether.

2. The Enterprise Must Realize and Believe That It Could Not Stand Solely on Its Own without a Proactive Sales Effort

This factor is also predicated on the salesforce's being profitable or at least having the chance to be. Assuming that it is profitable, the organization as a whole must wholeheartedly accept and internalize the belief that the organization could not exist without the day-to-day results and value delivered by the salesforce.

In cases where the sales effort is merely one part of the overall revenue generation machinery of the organization, it may be necessary to articulate and communicate the proper role and percentage of revenue that the salesforce should represent.

The real secret, however, is to ensure that every team member accomplish things that the organization respects. In the final analysis, businesses are no different from any other team when it comes to respecting shared commitment.

3. The Sales Department Must Be Championed by a Well-Placed Set of Internal Constituencies That Support the Sales Effort without Equivocation

Unfortunately, there are many organizations whose sales departments have failed this test over the years. Where this occurred, it is not unusual to see that senior executives in the organization either did not rise to their positions of leadership from the sales ranks, don't support the sales effort, or simply do not understand it.

Let me provide a classic example. For a number of years, we worked on and off with a manufacturing organization that is well known in the furniture industry. The CEO is a brilliant guy who attended one of the most prestigious universities in the country. He made his mark in the financial arena and was promoted through the accounting ranks to be CEO. His climb through the ranks tells you that this organization does not see itself primarily as a sales-driven organization.

After a continuous series of false starts, we began to make significant progress in terms of upgrading and enhancing the sales team. However, time after time, we would get to the point where everything was ready to move forward only to be stonewalled again and again by the CEO. His sales executives were frustrated, the salespeople disappointed, and the best intentions of all of us were dashed. In the final analysis, he couldn't understand why salespeople needed training, believing that sales was something that should be intuitive; that simply by building better products, customers would flock to buy them; and that incentives, pricing strategy, marketing, promotions, and programs would rule the day—not sales.

Unfortunately, example after example of that same scenario plays out repeatedly. However, there are just as many examples of situations where well-placed executives or highly influential ones were able to position the salesforce well internally and exercise the influence needed to enhance their positioning in the organization. Some even positioned the entire enterprise as a totally sales-driven organization. As a consequence, the sales team was properly supported, funded, and successful. In the final analysis, success is often driven to the level and amount of internal support you receive. By attracting and nurturing the internal support you need to be successful, the long-term viability of any group is guaranteed. A salesforce is no different.

4. The Sales Department Must Be Well Managed by Respected Managers and Exceed Minimal Performance Standards

This principle finds its roots in the truth that people in organizations respect and admire others who are held to the same or, ideally, higher standards than they themselves are held to as a measure of performance.

You need to look no further than the military to verify this reality. The Army has its Special Forces; the Navy, its Seals. No one questions the discipline handed out by a Marine gunnery sergeant or the skill required to be an Air Force fighter pilot. The same is true with civilian organizations. The sales team has to be admired, respected, and tightly managed. There must be standards of performance that exceed the general standards set in the overall organization.

This is especially true if the income potential for members of the sales team exceeds what others in the organization can earn, which is quite often the case. How they are coached to interface, cooperate with, and coordinate activities with other people and departments across the entire enterprise is also a part of those standards.

It is not unusual for sales managers to find themselves coaching sales team members on how to better communicate with other staff members. They frequently find themselves acting to resolve conflicts and let other people in the organization know that they have taken decisive corrective action, established tighter procedures, set higher standards, or demanded a superior level of performance from sales team members.

Make your sales team like the Green Berets, Marines, or Seals. You, they, and your entire organization will be better off for it.

5. Members of the Sales Department Must Interface with Other Departments Favorably

Being aggressive is important to sales success. However, this aggressiveness sometimes plays itself out in the wrong ways. For example, salesperson A commits to an early delivery date. That same salesperson then promises the customer that the delivery schedule can be adhered to without concern for other commitments, problems, or scheduled deliveries. Now the delivery department has a problem. Salesperson B loudly complains to her customer about the shoddy repair work done on his equipment. Now the service department has a problem. Salesperson C becomes overly aggressive with the accounting department so that his billings will go out ahead of schedule to speed up his commission check. Now the accounting department has a problem. Unfortunately, the sales manager for all these people has three separate problems.

Smart salespeople know that there are times to be more accommodating than demanding, more persuasive than pushy, and more sensitive than autocratic.

This situation occurs commonly in organizations that have one or two superstar salespeople who know they are important to the organization's success, know they deliver a huge amount of business, and, unfortunately, believe they are untouchable. Smart companies simply don't allow this sort of thing to occur. They understand that systems, rules, and procedures are important. Smart companies do their best to ensure that all salespeople comply with all standards.

6. The Sales Department Must Bring Collateral Value to the Enterprise

This collateral value is far more than just sales volume. Instead, it means bringing a sense of contribution, enrichment, and enhanced participation. Smart companies know that the sales team can play a significant role in tactical marketing, product development and research, troubleshooting, and enhanced customer service.

To bring this value to the enterprise, however, the sales department must be led from a perspective of participation rather than isolation, from the perspective of cooperation rather than competition, and from a perspective that says everyone is in this thing together and it is not in anyone's best interest to form an iconoclastic entity that exists solely for its own benefit. The sales team must truly believe that it is part of a symbiotic relationship between them and other departments and that, together, they all exist for the mutual benefit of one another.

7. The Members of the Sales Department Must Mesh Culturally with Enterprisewide Standards of Performance, Decorum, and Behavior

Salespeople and sales departments don't exist in a void. Every organization in the world is made up of people. And, like any human enterprise, every company has its own written rules of conduct, behavior, style, and manners. Salespeople need to understand what those standards are and comply with them.

For example, we have a client whose salespeople visit the home office only two to three times per year. The rest of the time they are operating out of offices in their homes. Unfortunately, the sales director had overlooked the importance of telling them the unwritten "rules of the road" that exist in the office. As a rule, the office is a rather quiet, reserved operation. Workers are very protective of their property, cubicles, and phones. They follow very strict guidelines relative to protocol and communication.

The sales director now knows that unless he reminds the sales team of these standards of performance every time there is a meeting, there is total chaos. Before he knew to take the appropriate action, salespeople would loudly and happily greet one another, use any available phone to call prospects or customers, and have a boisterously good time. How was that greeted? How do you think the sales team was described when out of earshot? How much proactive cooperation do they receive from the internal support staff?

8. The Sales Department Must Be Made Up of Competent, Capable, High-Performance-Oriented People

Sales is too important to allow incompetent, uncaring, or poor-performing salespeople to languish very long. Sales is a contact sport. It is also a bottom line sport. Salespeople who don't contact prospects or customers and/or don't sell shouldn't be in sales. It's that simple.

Other areas are more process oriented and allow people to hide for long time periods, but sales cannot be like that. This is particularly true as you look at the cash demanding realities that exist in the twenty-first century.

The sales culture in any organization must be one that is highly demanding, is rigorous to be a part of, and rewards performance, not promises. It reveals sales, not sulking; results, not rationalizing. Build a sales culture on the pillars of performance, and it will be one that is admired and respected both inside and outside the organization.

Job Coaching and Performance Management

Let's look at the TriMetrix Job Coaching and Performance Management System©[1] for a sample sales position that we recently benchmarked. It required these attributes:

1. Results orientation.
2. Influencing others.
3. Self-management.
4. Goal achievement.
5. Interpersonal skills.
6. Problem-solving ability.
7. Decision making.

The following motives are rewarded:

1. Utilitarian/economic.
2. Traditional/regulatory.
3. Theoretical.

The following behaviors are required:

1. Frequent interaction with others.
2. Versatility.
3. Frequent change.

These factors need to be evaluated in terms of a person's capacity to perform at any level that will be acceptable in this sales position:

---

[1] TriMetrix Job Coaching and Performance Management System, ©2003, Bill Brooks and Bill Bonnstetter.

Attributes

1. Results orientation.
   (a) Maintaining focus on goals.
   (b) Identifying and acting on removing potential obstacles to successful goal attainment.
   (c) Implementing thorough, effective plans and applying appropriate resources to produce results.
   (d) Following through on all commitments to achieve results.
2. Influencing others.
   (a) Effectively impacting others' actions.
   (b) Gaining commitment from others to achieve desired results.
   (c) Analyzing others' opinions and leading them to understand and willingly accept desired alternatives.
   (d) Persuading others in a positive manner.
3. Self-management.
   (a) Independently pursuing business objectives in an organized and efficient manner.
   (b) Prioritizing activities as necessary to meet job responsibilities.
   (c) Maintaining the required level of activity toward achieving goals without direct supervision.
   (d) Minimizing work flow disruptions and time wasters to complete high-quality work within a specified time frame.
4. Goal achievement.
   (a) Establishing goals that are relevant, realistic, and attainable.
   (b) Identifying and implementing required plans and milestones to achieve specific business goals.
   (c) Initiating activity toward goals without unnecessary delay.
   (d) Staying on target to complete goals regardless of obstacles or difficult circumstances.

5. Interpersonal skills.

   (a) Initiating and developing business relationships in positive ways.

   (b) Successfully working with a wide range of people at varying levels of the organization.

   (c) Communicating with others in ways that are clear, considerate, and understandable.

   (d) Demonstrating ease in relating to a diverse range of people of varying backgrounds, ages, experience, and education levels.

6. Problem-solving ability.

   (a) Analyzing all data relative to a problem.

   (b) Dividing complex issues into simpler components to achieve clarity.

   (c) Selecting the best options available to solve specific problems.

   (d) Applying all relevant resources to implement suitable solutions.

7. Decision making.

   (a) Analyzing data necessary for decision making.

   (b) Making major decisions impacting strategic outcomes appropriately and effectively.

   (c) Making decisions in a timely manner.

   (d) Demonstrating an ability to make unpopular and difficult decisions when necessary.

Values and Motives

1. Utilitarian/economic.

   (a) Understanding and valuing the economic needs of the organization.

   (b) Being practical, results oriented, and bottom line in thought and action.

    (c) Being concerned with the financial security of the organization.

    (d) Actively seeking new ways to generate revenue.

2. Traditional/regulatory.

    (a) Respecting company policies and procedures.

    (b) Incorporating organizational rules and regulations into business decisions.

    (c) Advocating adherence to company rules and regulations.

    (d) Respecting company culture and traditions.

3. Theoretical.

    (a) Actively seeking learning opportunities.

    (b) Staying up-to-date on industry developments.

    (c) Spending time and energy learning about unfamiliar topics.

    (d) Valuing and respecting the pursuit of knowledge.

Behaviors

1. Frequent interaction with others.

    (a) Being friendly when interrupted by another person.

    (b) Dealing easily with others.

    (c) Being people oriented rather than task oriented.

    (d) Demonstrating an enjoyment of dealing with people.

2. Versatility.

    (a) Displaying optimism in the face of change.

    (b) Being willing to adapt to changing assignments.

    (c) Demonstrating a willingness to accept abrupt change.

    (d) Demonstrating versatility under pressure.

3. Frequent change.

    (a) Being enthusiastic about working on a variety of tasks in a given time period.

    (b) Multitasking easily.

(c) Being adaptable.

(d) Championing change.

These measurable expectations are far more than judging salespeople solely on how many of what they have sold. In many ways, they define the sales culture. In reality, that culture is defined by the job. No one would agree that a certain sales volume is the necessary and, in some ways, final measure of a salesperson's performance. However, if salespeople fail to comply with the attributes, values, and behaviors that a job requires, there is a good chance that their sales performance will suffer along with it. By the same token, if they sell well, but fail to deliver the personal skills that the job demands, there is a great chance that these are people who are difficult to manage, likely have trouble with others in the organization, are considered "high maintenance," and need to be coached, counseled, and mentored extensively.

If you fail to hold every salesperson to an acceptable standard, there is a great chance that the entire department will not be well regarded. However, if you do, you will have established a sales culture that has standards of performance and accountability that guarantee performance—one that is widely respected across the entire enterprise. And that is important in a smart selling company.

CHAPTER 7

THE SUPERIOR SELLING CHAPTER REVIEW

- Certain factors must be present or developed so that a solid sales culture can flourish.
- As a general rule, organizations can be defined as having a primary orientation toward:

Marketing.

Sales.

Distribution.

Service.

Operations.

Manufacturing.

Research and development.

Engineering.

Hospitality.

- Many organizations don't know what they are. As a result, they have a climate of competing cultures, an environment where different departments are battling for attention.

- Should you choose to define yourself as a sales-driven company, the following eight factors must be firmly entrenched:

Factor 1: The sales department must be profitable.

Factor 2: The enterprise must realize and believe that it could not stand solely on its own without a proactive sales effort.

Factor 3: The sales department must be championed by a well-placed set of internal constituencies that support the sales effort without equivocation.

Factor 4: The sales department must be well managed by respected managers and have performance standards that exceed even the most demanding standards of other departments.

Factor 5: Members of the sales department must interface with other departments favorably.

Factor 6: The sales department must bring value to the enterprise.

Factor 7: The members of the sales department must mesh culturally with enterprisewide standards of performance.

Factor 8: The sales department must be composed of competent, capable, high-performance-oriented people.

- Strong accountability will define the culture. And that culture must be well regarded and respected enterprisewide.

Accountability

Accountability Really Pays

What, exactly, is *accountability?* Ask a thousand people this question and you'll likely get hundreds of different answers.

Whatever the answers, most somehow revolve around results, perhaps how close or far salespeople are from sales quotas or whether they exceed a goal or reach a predetermined plateau representing some sort of finish line or level of achievement with a standard to be met. The problem with this scenario? All of that achievement is just too little, too late.

In some cases, organizations are a little more sophisticated and define the key factors that eventually lead to a sale as being the primary things that salespeople should be accountable for *doing.* For example, generating leads, making sales calls, giving presentations, and earning referrals are things salespeople should *do.* This is a more refined definition than broadly saying a salesperson should merely "achieve a predetermined sales result." However, most still haven't dug far enough into the real issues that define the fundamental behaviors, actions, and activities that determine the effectiveness with which a sales-person goes about the business of gaining those opportunities, seeking the referrals, and making presentations. Those issues include activities that ultimately determine whether their sales results are good, bad, or mediocre; attributes, motives, and behaviors that are defined when the job is benchmarked; the standards that are determined when hiring a salesperson; and the performance expectations that are evaluated as explained in the previous chapter. Accountability requires all of these and more.

Let's take one more look at what accountability means in its most fundamental sense: being held answerable for your own behaviors, actions, and results.

To be held to this standard, smart sales organizations have certain factors in place. Without these factors, you will never be able to hold anyone accountable or answerable for their behaviors, actions, and results:

- *Responsibility:* The obligation to perform the duties required of the sales position.
- *Authority:* The right to act within given parameters with available resources.

Let's examine the downside of what happens when the right combination of these two factors is not in place—when either or both are not present at the levels that guarantee optimum sales performance (see Figure 8.1).

Cell 1

Salespeople are very limited in both their level of responsibility and authority. For example, they have little or no responsibility for all phases of the sales effort. They have little or no authority to handle pricing issues, issue credits, service accounts, authorize returns, or resolve problems. The result? A powerless

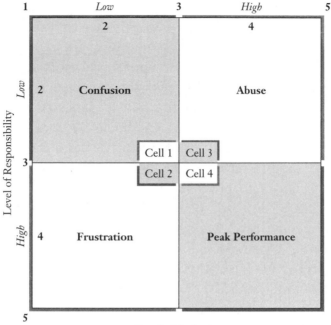

FIGURE 8.1 The Responsibility and Authority Matrix

salesforce that performs at only a fraction of its total capacity. This is a disaster waiting to happen, a situation where there is abysmal commitment and total confusion.

Cell 2

In this scenario, salespeople are given a higher level of responsibility. They are charged, for example, with all of the sales-related activity in a territory or with handling every phase of a project or sales plan. However, when it comes to the level of authority to expend a predetermined amount of money or to commit resources, they are limited. The result is frustration as they constantly have to check with someone else to provide timely answers to customers' issues, refunds, solve problems, or to commit available resources. This creates yet another "paper tiger" syndrome—people who look and act as though they can make things happen but lack the level of authority to do so.

We have heard salespeople hundreds of times over the years complaining bitterly about this type of situation. It's the same old refrain, "I'm told that I'm 100 percent responsible for what goes on in my territory . . . but when it comes time to answer customers' problems, spend a few bucks to make customers happy, answer their questions about future commitments, negotiate price, modify terms, or make a corporate commitment, I have no authority to provide any answers." The other part of what we hear? "I'm sick of it." The result? Frustration. And great salespeople leave. Average or poor ones stay and just ride it out for 20 to 30 years or as long as they have to. They "quit and stay" or "retire in place." If you believe that many organizations refuse to put up with this, look around. They do. Particularly if they want to have salespeople who won't rock the boat. You may even want to look at your own organization.

Cell 3

In this scenario, salespeople are literally allowed to run wild. They have complete authority relative to budgets, use of staff resources, access to support, promises, referrals, pricing, margins, terms, and more. When it comes time to assume responsibility for the consequence of those actions, however, it falls on someone else's shoulders. The classic case might look something like this:

SALES MANAGER: Who authorized the 12 percent discount?

SALESPERSON: I did. Remember, I have been authorized to negotiate everything.

SALES MANAGER: Who will explain this to my boss?

SALESPERSON: That's your responsibility. All you told me was that I could negotiate price, and I assumed that you were responsible for explaining what I did.

The result here, unfortunately, is abuse. Think about this for just a moment. What would a 5-year-old child do if he or she could eat all the candy in the world and had unlimited authority to buy more every day?

In the context of sales, a salesperson needs to sell a certain number of products or a specific level to service quarterly to hit a quota. However, the marketplace is tough. As a concession, all that is required of salespeople is to sell more. They are free to negotiate any price, promise any service level, and commit whatever resource is needed to keep the account, and they have an unlimited checkbook to make the customer happy. But here's the better news. You take full responsibility for whatever happens. The salesperson doesn't need to worry about anything relative to budgets, margins, or commitments. You'll take care of that.

What would happen? That should be obvious. Pure abuse—abuse of power, limits, and resources. Low levels of responsibility coupled with high levels of authority doesn't breed a paper tiger. Instead, it cross breeds an aggressive, misuse of resources coupled with a ready-made retreat from any sense of obligation to perform.

Cell 4

Smart companies and smart sales executives operate in this cell. Unfortunately, it is not as easy to be in that space as it may first appear because most organizations have trouble quantifying and communicating the real, tangible, measurable levels of responsibility and authority that are given to someone. What do Level 3 responsibility and Level 5 authority look like?

For example, what is *a lot* of authority? What is *a little?* What are equal levels of responsibility and authority? The trick is to define, as clearly as possible, what the parameters of both are for the salesperson.

Let's look at some examples. We have a client in the construction industry that empowers salespeople with total responsibility for selling their product to certain industries, where each salesperson is highly qualified and universally well regarded. With that significant level of responsibility (the obligation to perform) goes a high level of authority (the right to act), which means that salespeople have the authority to:

- Negotiate price up to an agreed-on discount.
- Authorize service work to be done on equipment up to an agreed-on level.
- Commit customer service/support resources to solve customer problems up to a certain number of people and for an agreed-on time period.

By the same token, we have other clients who give limited responsibility to their salespeople. They then couple that with an equally limited level of authority. For example, salespeople are responsible for obtaining leads, identifying qualified prospects, and selling accounts. Once the new account is earned, it is turned over to customer retention/service specialists whose job is to guarantee retention. Salespeople are responsible for new sales only.

This group of salespeople has limited authority. They cannot negotiate price, commit corporate resources, or authorize service. However, they can approach their appropriate manager, who can approve discounts up to a certain percent and authorize terms if necessary.

What You Don't Want

As a sales leader, you don't want any of these to occur with your sales team:

- Confusion.
- Frustration.
- Abuse.

Provide the Sales Team with the Right Level of Responsibility

The answer? Be 100 percent sure that you provide your sales team with the level of responsibility commensurate with the authority that is needed given the realities of the sales position in question. Let's look at the levels:

Responsibility (the obligation to perform)

> Total—Level 5.
> Partial—Level 3.
> Limited—Level 1.
> None—Zero.

Authority

> Total—Level 5.
> Partial—Level 3.
> Limited—Level 1.
> None—Zero.

Areas where the levels of both responsibility and authority need to be defined and clarified include:

- Prospecting.
- Territory management.
- Positioning.
- Making appointments.

- Confirming appointments.
- Completing the sales cycle.
- Data gathering.
- Data entry.
- Data maintenance.
- Servicing accounts.
- Vertically integrating accounts.
- Account management.
- Discounts/price concessions.
- Volume pricing.
- Commitment of technical support.
- Product modification.
- Customer ownership.
- Budgets (travel, entertainment, etc.).
- Rebates.
- Lead acquisition cost.
- Personal use of company property (vehicles, computers, etc.).

In the final analysis, responsibility and authority are at the very core of accountability. If these are not assigned in clear and equal levels, the entire sales organization is in store for a whole host of problems. These two issues must be clarified first for any sales effort to be successful.

However, it doesn't stop there. This responsibility and authority issue extends to the sales management team as well. In fact, the real paper tigers are sales executives who have been given the responsibility to lead and manage the sales team but have been given a level of authority inconsistent with the level of responsibility that the position carries.

A Real-World Example

A sales executive was hired as president of a national sales organization with more than 3,500 salespeople disbursed in all 50 states. He was offered the position at high salary with liberal bonuses and benefits. He accepted it with the full belief and, as it turns out, false expectation that he had both the responsibility for all facets of the sales organization (selection, standards, pay plans, training, management, marketing, etc.) and the level of authority required to drive sales performance (bonus dollars, discretionary selection of sales managers, use of company plane, assigning of staff, salary discretion, etc.).

This executive was given all the legitimate responsibility he expected. However, the appropriate level of authority was woefully lacking. He told me that time after time, he would meet with field salespeople or managers, listen to their suggestions or problems, and then not have the full authority to act on their accurate, valid requests or suggestions. There were scores of times that he felt like a hypocrite as he would travel in the field, hold group feedback sessions, and know full well that he couldn't implement any of the changes that he, and the field, knew needed to be done.

The results were disastrous. He quickly lost any credibility with the field, who quickly picked up that he had great intentions but, unfortunately, no power. After a short time period, the stress of the situation simply got to be too much. He was embarrassed and ashamed of his inability to improve the organization. He looked as though he had aged years in only six or seven months. He left the job, went somewhere else, and flourished.

Was he a poor manager? An ineffective executive? If so, why was he so successful before he was recruited to the position (if he weren't, he never would have been hired in the first place) and then went on to even greater success after he left?

It was the unmatched levels of responsibility and authority that caused the problem. He had a very significant level of responsibility, coupled with an abysmally low level of authority for the position. Sales executives, too, must be sure that they have the appropriate and equal levels of both to be accountable for their performance and the performance of their sales team. If you miss this essential piece for your salespeople and yourself, both you and your sales team are doomed. Smart companies take the time to assign and clearly communicate the levels of responsibility and authority their salespeople and sales managers have.

Your Pay Plan and Accountability

Smart companies ensure that a salesperson's pay plan contribute significantly to his or her capacity for accountability. In any strong, smart, and high-performing sales organization, the pay plan helps to drive whatever it is that the organization wants to happen. It's another way to hold salespeople accountable in a very objective, straightforward way.

Whether it is higher margin sales, higher volume sales, or increased sales of a certain product or service, an effective pay plan can drive accountability. In the final analysis, whatever is sold by any sales organization should, somehow, be tied to the pay plan.

Smart companies know that this is a reality and create pay plans that drive to this inevitable end. Sales organizations that offer base salaries with no incentive end up where it is totally predictable they will. Remember the analogy of paying peanuts and getting monkeys? These organizations have a self-satisfied, falsely arrogant group of salespeople who know that no matter how well or poorly they sell, they will be well paid. On the other end of the spectrum is the commission-only gang, the organizations who believe that salespeople should be paid only if something is sold.

This latter group is just as erroneous in their thinking as are the salary-only proponents. Examples include the organization that offers commission only or three-week draw for a job that requires a salesperson six months to learn or the organization that hires salespeople on a pure draw versus commission plan for the first three months, only to discover that no one can sell anything for the first six months—and then wonders why they can't recover the draws from anyone. It's simple. People who have no money can't repay debts.

Our experience tells us that a pay plan that allows new salespeople to take the time to learn, assimilate, and apply the knowledge they need to have to succeed is best, followed by a blended plan that includes a base salary that rewards salespeople for doing those things necessary to be a productive part of the team. Couple that with a commission or bonus plan based on their personal performance, and you are very close to having a pay plan that fuels championship performance.

In the final analysis, salespeople's pay plans should reflect their abilities to deliver the outcomes, behaviors, sales, margin, and volume that are required. This type of plan feeds the accountability culture that is so essential to the development of a superior sales team that smart companies must have.

By the same token, great salespeople do want to be held accountable for what they do or deliver. Super achievers don't hide from the facts. Instead, they want them at the forefront and want to be rewarded for what they do. That's accountability at its best.

CHAPTER 8
THE SUPERIOR SELLING CHAPTER REVIEW

- Accountability, in its most fundamental sense, means being held answerable for your own behaviors, actions, and results.

- In some cases, organizations are more sophisticated and define the key factors that eventually lead to a sale as the things that salespeople should be accountable for *doing*.

- Certain factors must be in place to have true accountability:

  Factor 1: *Responsibility: The obligation to perform the duties required of the sales position.*

  Factor 2: *Authority: The right to act within given parameters with available resources.*

- As a sales leader, you don't want any of these three to occur with your sales team:

  Confusion.

  Frustration.

  Abuse.

- You need to be 100 percent sure that you provide your sales team with the level of responsibility (obligation to perform) that is commensurate with the authority (the right to act) needed given the realities of the sales position in question.

- Areas where the levels of both responsibility and authority need to be clarified include:

  Prospecting.

  Territory management.

  Positioning.

  Making appointments.

  Confirming appointments.

  Completing the sales cycle.

  Data gathering.

  Data entry.

  Data maintenance.

  Servicing accounts.

  Vertically integrating accounts.

  Account management.

Discounts/price concessions.

Volume pricing.

Commitment of technical support.

Product modification.

Customer ownership.

Budgets (travel, entertainment, etc.).

Rebates.

Lead acquisition cost.

Personal use of company property (vehicles, computers, etc.).

■ In the final analysis, responsibility and authority are at the very core of accountability. If these are not assigned in clear and equal levels, the entire sales organization is in store for a host of problems.

■ The most vulnerable paper tigers are sales executives who have been given the responsibility to lead and manage the sales team but have been given a level of authority that is inconsistent with the level of responsibility the position carries.

■ Smart companies ensure that salespeople's pay plans contribute significantly to their capacity for accountability.

■ A pay plan that allows new salespeople to take the time to learn, assimilate, and apply the knowledge they need to have to succeed is best.

■ Salespeople's pay plans should reflect their abilities to deliver the outcomes, behaviors, sales, margin, and volume that are required.

Integrating Marketing, Sales, and Service for Superior Performance

This chapter discusses how the sales department interacts with other departments in your organization and how these departments should interact with the sales team as well.

Some people still don't know the difference between marketing and sales or don't see any real connection between the two in the first place. Others believe that either (1) marketing drives the engine, or (2) they have already successfully integrated their organization's marketing, sales, and service efforts.

Examples of where the latter didn't happen include a client who embarked on an entire campaign based on rebates and promotions and forgot to tell the salesforce about it. Another initiated a premature campaign with a new product and had the sales team aggressively selling it only to find glitches in the product that couldn't be serviced and then permanently recalled it. A client released a new product but failed to have the service department order parts for any defective, new products.

Remember the embarrassment issue for salespeople? How about the problems that the service people had to deal with as they tried to resolve false promises?

Another example that most anyone can identify with is the car dealer who advertises that his dealership's service quality by assuring you that the service on your new car will be done correctly, the first time, every time. And he really believes it. Yet, when you have your vehicle serviced, it is far from what was promised.

This whole issue centers on the words *promise*, *expectations*, and *experience*. These words are so important that they are used as the core of this chapter. Your prospects and customers receive a *promise* concerning:

- Marketing.
- Sales.
- Service.

However, "promise" quickly translates into "expectation" as it relates to the upcoming sales and service experiences. For example, a marketing promise could be, "We're the no hassle, easy-to-deal-with car dealership." The customer then expects that level of treatment. However, the sales *experience* could be one of being hassled, and the service *experience* could be one of being difficult to deal with for repairs. Perhaps that is why the old tongue-in-cheek definition of marketing is "where the tires hit the clouds" whereas sales is "where the tire hits the road." Service is fixing the tire!

One definition deals with image, positioning, and attraction while the others (sales and service) are in the trenches, face-to-face with prospects and customers charged with matching the expectations and actual experience against the promise. Perhaps that is why former President Lyndon Johnson once quipped, "It is far easier to throw a grenade than it is to catch it." How right he was.

It is precisely because of words such as *promise, expectations,* and *experience* that the marketing, sales, and service efforts must be as integrated as possible.

However, sales departments aren't necessarily guilt free in this entire episode, either. Because of old-school selling, poor sales management, a flawed pay plan, or poor or inadequate training, a salesperson can fully understand what the expectations of customers are but be either unable or unwilling to deliver an experience that matches that expectation. The same could be true for service or delivery departments. Figure 9.1 is a diagram of this scenario.

What creates an unhappy customer? When any one of the three don't fully integrate or, at least, don't intersect at a reasonable level. Figure 9.2 shows an example.

In this case, the marketing promise and sales experience were fairly consistent. However, the services experience was inconsistent with the promises of both the sales and marketing efforts. Each interaction with each department creates this Promise–Expectation–Experience chain of events. And it occurs repeatedly with both new and existing customers. Do your expensive marketing efforts promote something that

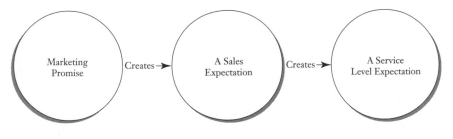

FIGURE 9.1   The Promise–Expectation Chain

FIGURE 9.2 Marketing and Sales Experience Connect and Service Experience Misaligns

your existing customers have already experienced as being untrue or unmet?

In Figure 9.3, the sales experience and service experience were closely integrated. However, the expectation that the prospect had for the sales and service experience didn't match the marketing promise and subsequent expectation. If the sales or service experience was good, perhaps the marketing promise just didn't match the expectations and established a set of expectations that were easily exceeded. And, if the theory holds true that good marketing makes a product or service successful regardless of the quality of the salespeople (I happen to disagree

FIGURE 9.3 Marketing Promise Misaligns with Sales and Service Experience

with that theory vehemently, by the way), it makes little difference what type of experience they have anyway.

If marketing's role is to attract the right prospects, position a product or organization, promote awareness, and do so in the right places to attract qualified prospects at the right price point, it would make sense to have those who are attracted be treated in a way that is consistent with the promise. If not, it could be disastrous.

If the product or service is positioned as basic, low priced, transactional, and marginal in value, there is nothing wrong with a sales approach that meets that expectation. In fact, it could be argued that it should. That's why there is a big difference between the wait staff at Joe's Hamburger Grill and the five-star restaurant at a posh resort. It's all about promise, expectation, and experience.

Figure 9.4 shows the ultimate fiasco. Here, nothing connects. It would take a pretty desperate prospect to buy from this organization. In this case, no one is talking to anyone else in the organization. The marketing department has not had its message communicated to the sales team. The service department has not gotten the sales or marketing message. The marketing department and service department have not connected, and the sales team hasn't connected with either.

FIGURE 9.4   **Total Disconnect**

FIGURE 9.5 Integration and Total Connection

In this case, the prospects interfacing with the salespeople either have expectations that are unmet or exceeded wildly (who knows which?), and those who do buy have the same experience with the service department.

The result is an inconsistent, poorly defined strategy across the entire organization, an organization fraught with finger pointing, blame, denial, backbiting, slippery revenues, reduced cash flow, and, likely, even extinction. Would you care to bet on the success they're having with the retention of customers? And, as you know, the secret to long-term business survival and success is dependent on the number of customers you can retain, vertically integrate, use as referral source, and create as unpaid salespeople for your enterprise.

Figure 9.5 shows the ideal scenario.

The more these three areas overlap, the better off you are. Smart organizations do their best to ensure that the promise–expectation–experience chain is never broken. In fact, they do their best to ensure that the chain is more than unbroken and the links overlap and are totally integrated. Marketing, sales, and service are all on the same page. (Service could relate to delivery, technical support, internal operations, customer service, or any other group of people that interface with customers during or after the sale. Overlook incorporating these people into your marketing/sales team and you are destined for failure.)

Some Solutions

A good friend and client, Mike Delaney, uses an interesting term, *tactical marketing*. This is the placement of actual marketing tools and strategies into the hands of other departments that interface with prospects and customers while simultaneously expanding the marketing message.

However, Mike goes further than that. He believes that the entire marketing thrust, philosophy, direction, theme, and premise must be totally integrated and ingrained into the fiber of the entire enterprise. And he is right. The actual tools that practitioners use (sales aids, prospecting pieces, etc.) are nothing more than hands-on, operational items that are used to communicate the marketing message more clearly and succinctly.

Salespeople need to know precisely how their organization, products, and even they themselves should be positioned in the market. They must then be trained to be consistent with that image, for example:

- The most exclusive.
- The largest.
- The most approachable.
- The low-price leader.
- The street-smart solution provider.
- The technical leader.

- The most customer friendly.
- The most expensive.
- The choice of discriminating buyers.
- The 24-hour service provider.

For sake of discussion, it makes little difference what position you choose to take. What does make a difference is how well you communicate that position to all the internal constituencies who interface with prospects or customers. What is important is how effectively you are able to monitor, provide feedback, and course-correct those things that happen in the field.

Sales, marketing, and service departments must never operate in isolation. This happens far too often. The relationship among the three is, perhaps, the most essential thing that organizations and the people in them must build, nurture, and sustain.

Remember the organizations with competing cultures where each one is vying for leadership? Smart companies get past all of that silliness. They decide what the customer wants, how they want to see it, how they'll buy great amounts of it, and how they want it delivered and serviced. They make a bold promise that even exceeds that expectation and then do their best to exceed that lofty expectation.

It's not that easy, however. It requires that egos be set aside, communications be opened, and everyone work conscientiously and in consort with other departments. The problem is that too many people tend to operate only in their own self-interest. When that happens, the customer loses. And, in the long run, the organization loses, too.

Several years ago, we worked with a well-known high-tech firm that had a very good, high-demand product. In fact, it was in such high demand that there was often a 6- to 12-month waiting list just to get it. Their marketing was good. Their service was good. But there was a problem: Their sales team was often out of the loop concerning marketing initiatives. The marketing department never talked to the sales department. The sales department never talked to the marketing department.

Suddenly, their product became obsolete. They did all in their power to replace it with newer, more innovative creations. However, the real problem was that their customers didn't like the company. Many told salespeople that it was now "their turn" to make the company uncomfortable . . . to have them experience the same pain that customers had endured after years and years of product delays and demands placed on them for minimum order requirement and so on.

Perhaps this is an extreme example. The successful transfer of products or services from your warehouse to your customer's really does involve more than the sales department. It truly is a team effort.

Another example is the salesperson who is fearful of taking service or technical people on a sales call for fear that they will:

- Confuse the prospect.
- Cite too many features.
- Be too technical.
- Talk their way out of the sale.
- Not understand that there is a sales process.

Smart companies provide some form of minimal sales training for service and technical people. In the final analysis, these are the people who see more customers anyway. Wouldn't it make sense to teach them a few things that are essential? For example:

- The customer is important.
- The customer represents your paycheck.
- The customer will likely need to buy more of whatever it is you service.

Smart companies ensure that team selling follows a format and sequence. They ensure that whenever someone is on a sales call with a salesperson, both are on the same page at the same time. But here's a potential problem. What if the sales department has no linked, sequential process that is to be followed? How can anyone learn to follow something that doesn't exist? That's when you have salespeople and service or technical people stepping on each other's words, raising unnecessary objections, and generally ruining the sales call.

The Bottom Line

This whole situation can be resolved with one simple word. That word is one that is alien to sales. In fact, it is a word that is used more in oratory or theatre than it is anywhere else. The word is *segue*.

A segue is a transition. It's how you easily, smoothly, and with minimal effort move from one topic to another. In fact, in a great presentation, the segue is the vehicle that makes the whole presentation work. It's a way to tie different parts of a presentation, film, or production together with a seamless and effortless transition.

The transition from marketing to sales can best be done with Mike Delaney's *tactical marketing*. In today's marketplace, the very act of prospecting is really tactical marketing. The concept of pull prospecting versus push prospecting demands a marketing bent and a consistency of message. Precisely how salespeople position themselves needs to match the positioning of the enterprise and how it chooses to position its solutions.

Placing valuable and usable tools in the hands of salespeople should be an extension of the marketing message. The proper use of the tools themselves should also be an extension of the marketing message. The type of salespeople representing the organization is an extension of it. Even the types of cars they drive and the way they dress are an extension of it.

However, the segue is the key. How do you transition the marketing message in usable, practical, real-world ways for street-smart application to salespeople? That's the secret.

The same segue that was articulated between marketing and sales must also be made to the service department (and the delivery, parts, or any other department that interfaces with prospects or customers). And here's the problem.

These are the last people in the line. They need to understand the marketing promise and will become the beneficiaries of the sales experience. It is incumbent that salespeople exceed the expectations held for the sales experience or there will be automatic problems for those who follow.

If all of these constituencies do understand the overall direction and share a common understanding, however, the results can be fantastic.

Smart companies ensure that everyone who ever sees, talks with, associates with, or comes in contact with a prospect or customer understand exactly what the promise–expectation–experience chain is. They also understand how to ensure that the chain never breaks. They then work hard to create situations where everything matches.

CHAPTER 9

THE SUPERIOR SELLING CHAPTER REVIEW

■ Some organizations don't know the difference between marketing and sales or don't see any connection between the two in the first place.

- It is precisely because of words such as *promise, expectations,* and *experience* that the marketing, sales, and service efforts must be as integrated as possible.

- Because of old-school selling, poor sales management, a flawed pay plan, or inaccurately defined training, a salesperson can understand what the expectations of customers are but be either unable or unwilling to deliver an experience that matches the expectation that marketing has created.

- An inconsistent, poorly defined sales marketing and service strategy for the entire organization results in an organization fraught with finger pointing, blame, denial, backbiting, slippery revenues, and reduced cash flow.

- The more these three areas—sales, marketing, and service—overlap, the better off you are.

- The entire marketing thrust, philosophy, direction, theme, and premise must be totally integrated and ingrained into the fiber of the entire enterprise.

- Salespeople need to know precisely how their organization, products, and even they are positioned in the market. They must then be trained to be consistent with that image.

- Sales, marketing, and service departments must never operate in isolation.

- The successful transfer of products or services from your warehouse to your customer's really does involve more than the sales department. It truly is a team effort.

- Smart companies provide some form of minimal sales training for service and technical people.

- Smart companies ensure that team selling follows a format and sequence.

- The concept of pull prospecting versus push prospecting demands a marketing bent and a consistency of message.

- Placing valuable and usable tools in the hands of salespeople should be an extension of the marketing message.

- The segue is the key to transitioning the marketing message in usable, practical, real-world ways for street-smart application by salespeople.
- Smart companies ensure that everyone who ever sees, talks with, associates with, or comes in contact with a prospect or customer understand exactly what the promise–expectation–experience chain is.

Successful Product Introductions

A nother harsh reality of twenty-first century business is that you will never again be able to rest on the successes of existing products. The pressures of competition will increasingly mandate that new product releases, upgrades, updates, and wholesale product direction will likely be the rule far more than the exception.

It is also a reality that salespeople will be the ones who will take these new products to the doorsteps of prospects and customers. This is precisely why this Insider Secret is so essential for successful, smart selling.

And there are a number of things that are especially intriguing about those salespeople. Over the years, I have been involved in a great deal of research that proves just how intriguing salespeople can be. One of the more interesting is the work that I was a part of several years ago with the late Tom Travisano. Tom was a fantastic researcher and gifted consultant. He was a great writer and a fantastic friend. He is dearly missed by many people.

This research dealt with the role of what people want versus what they need when making buying decisions. The fundamental truth Tom initially advanced is that what people *want* is a far better predictor of what they will and won't buy than are many other factors—including what they actually need in any product or service.

What does that mean for a sales smart organization and its salespeople? Far more than anything else, salespeople do not *want* to be embarrassed in front of a prospect or customer. Salespeople may *need* a sale, but don't want to be embarrassed in the process of making it. As a consequence, this fear of embarrassment drives their performance in a multitude of ways, including:

- Reluctance to call on unhappy customers (there is no such thing as call reluctance; it is the fear of embarrassment that springs from being called to task by a dissatisfied customer).
- Resistance to call on demanding prospects.
- Hesitancy to use outdated selling skills that could, perhaps, be easily detected by prospects as transparent ploys or tactics.
- Overloading prospects with data to avoid being asked questions they can't answer.
- Not even wanting to have the title *salesperson* on a business card.

Perhaps the most critical reality is that this simple fear of embarrassment is also a major reason so many new products tend to languish, fail to take off, or fail to achieve the high expectations that were initially held for them. Expensive product launches are planned and executed. Elaborate marketing plans are funded with significant dollars. Fortunes are spent on marketing aids, sales aids, and tools. And the results are just average. Or worse, they are just plain terrible. And with customers wanting more new products coupled with your need to stay competitive in the marketplace, the stakes are high.

What can go wrong? In a surprisingly large number of cases, the salesforce is never trained in a way that allows them to feel confident in their understanding of the product. As a consequence, they fear being asked questions they can't answer. They aren't sure about the level of customer service or support that will or won't accompany the product. In some cases, they don't feel at ease when presenting their product (will this thing even do what it is supposed to do during the presentation?). They may be unclear about the warranty. They can be confused about availability dates for the product. In some cases, they aren't even sure how they are going to be compensated. In other cases, they may not even know when or how to stop selling the current product and how to start the new one in motion.

It is easy for organizations to say things such as:

- "We had a great launch video."
- "We brought all of them in and explained the whole thing."
- "It was a great meeting. They all seemed to be enthused about the new product."

The woeful truth is that most launch efforts involving salespeople are either too little, too late, or even worse, too much data, too late. The hidden magic is in being committed to spend more time with the training of the sales team on how to sell a new product than is spent on virtually any other phase of the introduction. And that is a little-known strategy among organizations that just don't sell smart.

I was working with a major international OEM several years ago when they launched a new and highly innovative product into the market. Their new product was an expensive piece of capital equipment with a $120,000 price tag. Before this product, they had been selling a much less expensive one that was a middle-of-the-road, rather unexciting offering.

Their new product was bigger, faster, and incorporated a more forward look in design that introduced a whole new level of complexity to the marketplace. It also required a totally different sales approach. My contact at the firm was the very bright and capable vice president of marketing, who entered the scene at a point after a soft landing had already occurred. He steadfastly insisted that the harder launch include a very heavy emphasis on teaching salespeople how to sell the new product, learn its value, and sell it against lower priced competitors. He demanded a full frontal attack incorporating the new product and precisely how to sell it.

Together, we launched an international effort toward on-going, meaningful sales training and education. For months, our training teams traveled North America and meticulously trained more than 850 salespeople on exactly how to sell the new product.

But that's not all. There were companion seminars geared toward product knowledge, hands-on training for salespeople to use the equipment, and presentations by finance and warranty staff from headquarters. This whole process preceded the hard launch, was simultaneous with it, and continued after it.

Was this an expensive undertaking? Yes, it was, until you start to analyze the results. It ended up being the most success-ful new product launch in the history of the company. It could have been the most successful in the history of their industry.

Within six months of the introduction, their product was voted the best in the industry. They gained more market share than ever in the history of their company. Our training program was voted as the best in the industry. Turnover of their sales-force dropped by double digits in one year because the sales-people were making money. Their dealers were successful, and the new product became the standard in the industry.

Why did all of that happen? Because their 850 salespeople knew their new product inside and out. They had confidence in their ability to present it with no hitches. They had confidence in the product. They knew the right questions to ask. They knew how to sell value. They could go toe-to-toe with anyone.

They knew the product would perform well and be serviced correctly. They had confidence that their customers would be totally pleased, serviced professionally, and would not be calling them with problems or difficulties over which they had no control.

On the other hand, there is a companion horror story I must share with you. This involved an organization that prided itself on innovation and responsiveness to the market. In fact, they could even be described as hyperresponsive to the market. The entrepreneurial CEO never ceased to believe that newer was always better. He also believed that more was better than little.

Being a creative entrepreneur, he spent much of his own personal time in research and development. As a result, he knew the intricate subtleties and every internal complexity of all products as they continued to roll off the production line in his ever-increasing torrent of innovation.

His mistake? He believed that he could give his sales team a quick overview of each of the products as they became available. The problem? The 30,000-foot overview was not enough to give the salespeople the level of confidence, understanding, belief, and depth they needed. He was frustrated and couldn't understand why his sales team would retreat to the old products and never seemed to jump on board with the new, innovative, and exciting products that his self-described creative genius had birthed.

The actions of his sales team were nothing more than symptoms. The real problem was much deeper. His sales team was even more frustrated than he was. They had gotten to the point that they hated to hear about new products. Then they got to a point that they didn't even listen. He was committed to the belief that each new innovation was going to be the big breakthrough they needed. Each would be the single new product that would turn them around, make them more competitive, and take them to a superior level of performance.

Ten Truths for Developing and Launching Products or Services

Based on these two true stories, let's look at 10 essential truths for developing and launching products or services successfully:

1. Don't introduce too many new products or services in too short a time.

2. Be sure you have worked out as many bugs as possible from mechanical or structural issues, delivery, pricing, warranty, and pay plan before you release the product.

3. Have all sales tools, aids, and marketing pieces totally completed and tested before the introduction.

4. Begin to train salespeople sufficiently before the introduction so that they can have adequate time to gain a comfortable level of product mastery.

5. Determine every feasible question that salespeople will be asked about the product so that they can be trained to respond.

6. Teach salespeople all you can about competition, comparison pricing, how the competition sells, and how you expect competition to respond to your new initiative.

7. Be flexible and ready to update, modify, or radically overhaul your product and support tools when you receive real-time, live feedback from the field.

8. Resist the temptation to deny facts or defend an indefensible position concerning the feedback you get from the field.

9. Continually modify your training methods as your product matures, faces competition, and your competition learns how to sell against your product, replicate it, or even improve it with their version.

10. Understand that your sales team will go through a series of plateaus, growth spurts, successes, and failures as they learn how to sell the product. Expect bumps and plateaus. Then build momentum.

Let's look at each of these in some detail.

1. Don't Introduce Too Many New Products or Services in Too Short a Time

For many salespeople, simple is better. Easy is better than difficult. Each product requires its own set of qualifying questions, unique presentation format, objections to be dealt with, and pricing issues to handle. Customers need to be given a better understanding of every product before they can comfortably buy it. All of these issues must be dealt with in a productive and comprehensive way. And that can't happen with a constant deluge of new offerings supported by a minimal training effort.

I was recently subjected to a sales presentation by a sales representative who was interested in selling a unique, novelty item for us to use in our conference center. On at least four occasions, he said, "I don't know much about this or that new item. We get so many new things, I can't stay on top of them all." Need I ask you what my reaction was? We haven't bought yet and he has not been back since. I still have no confidence that he was offering the best, most up-to-date products for us. By his own admission, he couldn't stay on top of his own products. And I was totally convinced that he could not solve any potential problem or service our account in any meaningful way.

You are far better scheduling releases in ways that allow them to be spaced for training, understanding, confidence, and competence to build. In the case of our novelty salesperson, we may have been interested in—or have a need for—one of his newer items. However, he didn't feel confident enough to even present them correctly to us. What a shame for him, his employer, and us.

2. Be Sure You Have Worked Out as Many Bugs as Possible from Mechanical or Structural Issues, Delivery, Price, Warranty, and Pay Plan before You Release the Product

This principle is reminiscent of the original movie, *Robocop*.[1] Released many years ago, it portrays a robotic police officer complete with automatic weapons, lasers, bombs, and everything in between. The new, high-tech breakthrough is introduced at an exclusive, boardroom presentation only to go completely awry. Bombs explode prematurely, weapons misfire, and laser-guided missiles launch by error. The room is destroyed, participants are scattered, and the product presentation totally fails.

Have you ever had this occur with your product? If so, it may not have been as extreme. I'll guarantee, however, that it appeared that way to the salesperson who made the presentation. To that person, the flawed presentation was just as traumatic and, in his or her mind, just as dramatic, too.

And here is the issue. How long will it be before that salesperson enthusiastically recommends and subsequently demonstrates that same product again? How about the next new one?

I have heard discussions over the years from salespeople who all say the same things when premature product releases occur, for example:

- "They haven't thought this thing through."
- "I don't know how this thing is going to work."
- "I wish the people who thought this product up would come out in the field and see how it is really received."

---

[1] *Robocop*, 1987, by MGM Studios.

- "I haven't even been told how I'll get paid on this new product."
- "I don't want to be responsible when this thing fouls up my customer's entire system."

This whole issue of premature product release has been fueled significantly by the rapid fire introduction of software products. The rationale in the software industry is that if they get it to market faster, they can always e-mail patches and then come out with version 2.0. Unfortunately, not all updates or improvements for other products are that easy. Nor are all customers that forgiving. They have not been trained to buy the way that software purchasers have been trained to make their purchases from the beginning. And, now, even software purchasers are tiring of being forced to keep buying expensive upgrades.

3. Have All Sales Tools, Aids, and Marketing Pieces Totally Completed and Tested before the Introduction

It was 1990. I had been invited to speak at the annual sales meeting of a well-known firm in the Midwest. Everyone in the crowd was visibly excited about the event. It had been a great year, profits were up, and the entire sales team had come to the meeting in good spirits.

They were particularly excited about the new product release and the powerful new sales aids they had been told would make their lives easier. I arrived early in the morning to prepare for my presentation. The firm's director of marketing was there, too. She was eagerly awaiting the arrival of the materials. She kept checking her watch. I could see that something was wrong—terribly wrong.

The materials finally arrived about 10 minutes before the event was to start. As she nervously opened the boxes, I could detect the strong odor of freshly applied ink. Apparently, the whole thing was a last-minute rush job from the printer, who had obviously worked overtime to get the materials finished for the launch meeting.

As I looked at the colorful brochures, sales aids, guides, and tools that spewed from the boxes, it became clear to me that there was a problem. None of it seemed to be coordinated. There were elaborate, complicated keys and charts to match products, options, and price points. It looked like a jigsaw puzzle.

The director of marketing understood the puzzle. The director of new product development did, too. The director of sales had some idea about how it worked. I had no idea at all. And about two hours later, none of the sales team did, either.

The new product portion of the meeting was a total disaster. The salespeople had many questions, but no one had any clear, direct answers. The tools had not been field-tested, run by any salespeople, shown to prospects, or simplified before they were released to the field. As happens in most situations like this, the decision was made at the meeting to "go ahead and use the materials we have developed until we need to upgrade them." A promise was made to "review how things work out" and then make "any changes that might be needed."

After several months of confusion and disarray, the materials were totally removed from the field. Prospects were confused, salespeople were upset, the new products didn't sell, and the whole thing proved to be a total disaster.

What caused it? A simple, but common error. Most of the focus was on the product and much was on the marketing. Very little, if any, was on tactical marketing or how it would be sold. Here's a recommendation. Start the process with this simple question: "How will this product be sold on the street?"

Start with that question. Don't end with it. Or, worse yet, don't be tempted to overlook it altogether. Salespeople need to have tools that are attention grabbing, user and customer friendly, easy and simple to use, and uncomplicated in execution. If you wait until the last minute or make it an afterthought, these tools will never meet that specification.

4. Begin to Train Salespeople Sufficiently before the Introduction So That They Can Have Adequate Time to Gain a Comfortable Level of Product Mastery

Remember the capital equipment manufacturer who broke all sales records with its new product? We started our training process six to eight months *before* the actual product was released. The people in the Midwest? A three-hour seminar to teach them how to use freshly printed tools.

Before you think to yourself, "I don't want anyone out there to know about our new product until it's released," you need to stop and think about the way things are in the real world. There is a good chance that your deep, dark secret has already gotten out of the bag somewhere, somehow, with somebody in your marketplace anyway. Besides, if your new product is that good, no one could ever replicate it, understand it, exceed it, or even begin to understand how to market and sell it in the comparatively short time frame you will need to train your sales team.

People don't develop mastery of any subject or topic quickly. It takes time, repetition, reinforcement, being held accountable, and real-world application before someone will truly understand something. But it doesn't always have to take months. However, you cannot gloss over this process either. Make the time commitment that is necessary.

Fortunately, with digital technology, it's relatively easy and affordable to train people. Your goal should be to ensure your salespeople have as much mastery over the new product as possible before it is released. Empower them with the knowledge and expertise they need to hit the streets running.

Those with mastery are the ones who are able to apply the right knowledge at precisely the right time to achieve a goal.

This could mean applying the right question at the right time, giving the right answer to a product question, or explaining precise warranty terms clearly. And you need to accelerate your salespeople to this mastery level as well as you can before the product is released if possible.

Research shows that to be performing at that mastery level, people must have a large amount of information and at some point make the transition so they automatically recognize patterns and instantly apply the right solutions at the right time. In a selling situation, salespeople who are novices with a product will think their way through several different responses and may eventually come up with the best one. In contrast, the master instantly recognizes the correct response and confidently delivers it.

Salespeople must first gain an initial understanding of the facts. This can be done through reading, lecture, seminar, web training, or teleseminars. This elementary level of understanding is important because it provides a framework for the salesperson to organize and create a mental map of the facts surrounding your new product.

Although that is not enough, unfortunately, that is where many organizations stop. The most difficult facts start to fade from memory within minutes. The easier facts fade and disappear over a few more days. To prevent this problem, the brain must work with the facts over a period of time. Research also shows that when there is fear ("learn this or else" or "this thing could embarrass me in front of the prospect"), the fight or flight syndrome sets in and people learn absolutely nothing as their brain simply shuts down.

We have initiated a breakthrough training process with our clients that is digitally based and accomplishes all of this and more. However, even that process requires time. You must do all you can to have your salespeople develop an early level of mastery over product knowledge and confidence in presenting your new product or service. If you fail to do that, they will hesitate to present it. In the worst case, they might even be resistant. Take the time. It will pay off.

5. Determine Every Feasible Question That Salespeople Will Be Asked about the Product So That They Can Be Trained to Respond

You don't want your salespeople merely to *react* to questions they receive about the new product. Instead, you want them to intelligently *respond*. The difference between these two similar terms is startling. Reaction is the visceral, emotional way of handling questions. Remember, it is the novice who mentally seeks answers from a plethora of choices and then grabs the closest sounding one for responding. The master implicitly knows how to respond in the most accurate, correct, persuasive, confident, and professional way.

Let's go back to the fundamental issue driving this whole phenomena. Salespeople do not want to be embarrassed in front of prospects or customers. Not knowing answers to pointed questions is, perhaps, the most fundamentally embarrassing situation there is for salespeople.

You need to spend a significant amount of time determining the most common questions salespeople will encounter. Remember that there are scores of questions that relate to your specific product. These 21 are merely suggestions for you to begin working with:

1. Why is this product better than the old one?
2. How long can I keep buying the current product, and will it stay in the inventory?
3. Does this mean any current product is obsolete?
4. Why did you sell me the old one if this new one was in development?
5. How will I switch to the new version?

6. What do I do about the remaining payments on the old model?

7. How much research and development went into this?

8. You told me how great the other one was—were you lying to me?

9. What type of guarantee do you offer me on this new one?

10. What happens if I don't like the new product? Will you take it back?

11. All of our people are comfortable with and trained on the old system. How are you going to help me train them? How much will the training cost?

12. When are you going to stop trying to sell me the latest and greatest?

13. You told me that the one I have was state-of-the-art. Why is this one better?

14. I heard that you are updating because you're having too many problems with the old model. Is that true?

15. How much field testing went into this? Is it fully functional?

16. What happens if this new model doesn't do what you say it will do?

17. Can you give me the names of some people who are using the new model? I'd like to talk with them.

18. I don't buy new and unproven things. What can you do to convince me that this is all you say it is?

19. Everybody tries to sell me untested things that have cost them a lot of money to build. Then I buy the first and "best" version and it doesn't perform up to expectations. Are you just trying to recover your investment by selling this to me?

20. This looks complicated. Can you explain it to me in simple terms?

21. I understand that your competition has a new model, too. How does yours compare?

Salespeople need to develop responses and learn precisely what to say. I am not suggesting any memorized script. I am, however, suggesting a formal, competent set of responses that reflects mastery and confidence. In the absence of this, you will have a new product introduction that is loaded with false starts, uncomfortable salespeople, and fewer presentations of the new product than is required for a successful introduction. You will have lousy sales, too.

6. Teach Salespeople All You Can about the Competition, Comparison Pricing, How the Competition Sells, and How You Can Expect Competition to Respond to Your New Initiative

There is little doubt that your competition is going to respond in some way to your introduction. Your salespeople need to know what they will do or at least have some idea about what they are most likely to do.

There is a very good chance that your competition knows that your new product is coming long before it is released in spite of your best efforts to keep everything under wraps.

After delivering well over 2,500 seminars, training sessions, and symposiums, it is still astounding that when I ask even experienced salespeople very fundamental questions about their competition, they simply don't know the answers. Often, what they appear to know is only rumor, innuendo, third-party anecdotal information, or just pure gossip. Silence comes when I ask them questions such as:

- What is the sales and marketing philosophy and strategy of your toughest competitor?

- How often do they call on prospects? Your current customers?
- Who, by name, do you compete against most often?
- What is their value proposition and how does it compare to yours?

I get blank stares and silence with those questions every time. What do you think I would get if I asked them more demanding questions such as:

- How will your competition counter your new product offering?
- Which of our weaknesses will they try to exploit?
- How will they respond in terms of pricing strategy?
- How soon will they bring a competitive product into the market?

7. Be Flexible and Ready to Update, Modify, or Radically Change Your Product or Support Tools When You Receive Real-Time, Live Feedback from the Field

To great salespeople, speed is important. And great salespeople are not interested in providing feedback that goes unheeded or appears to be dismissed altogether.

By the same token, your greatest source of meaningful, real-time data comes from the field. With all due respect to external marketing agencies or internal product development or marketing communications departments, the jury of last resort concerning the understanding and acceptance of your new product is the customer. And the ones most closely interfacing with prospects and customers are the salespeople. It's that simple.

You've moved far beyond focus groups and other structured events. You're now dealing with real-time, real responses from real people who are trying to sell a real product to real people who are considering whether they should buy it.

If the feedback says good things, improve those things. If it says mediocre things, act on them. If it says bad things, face it, make the changes and correct them fast.

8. Resist the Temptation to Deny Facts or Defend an Indefensible Position Concerning the Feedback You Get from the Field

This is more difficult than you might think, particularly if you have some sort of emotional connection to the product launch structure or the collateral tools that support it. It's not easy to accept that your best efforts are being rejected, is it?

Look at it from the perspective of the salespeople. They are the ones who are facing the wrath of prospects and customers daily. Don't defend. Act. And act now.

9. Continually Modify Your Training Methods as Your Product Matures, Faces Competition, and Your Competition Learns How to Sell against Your Product, Replicate It, or Even Improve It with Their Version

Your new product or service will face scrutiny, no matter how good it is. And the better it is, the more likely you'll face knock-off's, me-too's, and imitators by the bucketful. That mandates constant and consistent diligence to put stronger and better training in place. It also means constant monitoring of new tools to ensure that what you develop does answer the need that the field demands.

10. Understand That Your Sales Team Will Go through a Series of Plateaus, Growth Spurts, Successes, and Failures as They Learn How to Sell the Product. Expect Bumps and Plateaus. Then Build Momentum

Nothing is easy. That includes learning to sell something new. You will experience immense highs and disappointing lows. The secret is to prepare the sales team with as many tools and resources as possible. And then understand that even with the greatest preparation, it will not be easy.

Accept it, deal with it, and then have the tenacity and persistence to see each problem through and develop solutions to eliminate any future difficulties.

New product launches are not for the faint of heart. However, they are also a consistent theme in twenty-first century business. But if smart selling companies can prepare great salespeople with the best tools and training, new products can drive your organization to the next level. But it must be done right.

CHAPTER 10

THE SUPERIOR SELLING CHAPTER REVIEW

- What people *want* is a far better predictor of what they will and won't buy than are many other factors—including what they actually *need* in any product or service. As this century progresses, your customers will *want* product improvement, enhancements, and upgrades.

- Research has shown that far more than anything else, salespeople do not *want* to be embarrassed in front of a prospect or customer. Salespeople may need a sale but don't want to be embarrassed in the process of making it. As a consequence, this fear of embarrassment drives their performance in multitudes of ways.

- This simple fear of embarrassment is also a major reason so many new products tend to languish and fail to take off or achieve the high expectations that were held for them.

- Most launch efforts involving salespeople are either too little, too late, or even worse, too much data, too late.

- Ten essential truths to developing and launching products or services successfully are:

Truth 1: Don't introduce too many new products or services in too short a time.

Truth 2: Be sure you have worked out all the apparent bugs from mechanical or structural issues, delivery, pricing, warranty, and pay plan before you release the product.

Truth 3: Have all sales tools, aids, and marketing pieces completed and tested before the introduction.

Truth 4: Begin to train salespeople sufficiently before the introduction so that they can have adequate time to gain a comfortable level of product mastery.

Truth 5: Determine every feasible question that salespeople will be asked about the product so that they can be trained to respond.

Truth 6: Teach salespeople all you can about competition, comparison pricing, how the competition sells, and how you expect competition to respond to your new initiative.

Truth 7: Be flexible and ready to update, modify, or even radically overhaul your product and support tools when you receive real-time, live data from the field.

Truth 8: Resist the temptation to deny facts or defend an indefensible position concerning the feedback you get from the field.

Truth 9: Continually modify your training methods as your product matures, faces competition, and your competition learns how to sell against your product, replicate it, or even improve it with their version.

Truth 10: *Understand that your sales team will go through a series of plateaus, growth spurts, successes, and failures as they learn how to sell the product. Expect bumps and plateaus. Then build momentum.*

Sales Management and Selling Truths

Smart companies guarantee that the people they empower to be sales managers, leaders, or executives have a rich, deep, and solid understanding of what it takes to be an effective manager in a smart selling organization.

To be totally empowered, sales managers should master the knowledge that is contained in the previous 10 chapters. They also need to understand all of the Universal Sales Management Truths—101 proven principles that can be applied in any smart sales organization, anywhere, at any time. Note that the principles discussed earlier in this book are listed first; however, many more are just as valuable.

101 Universal Sales Management Truths[1]

1. Your organization will never be any stronger than the salespeople you recruit, select, and hire and how effectively they are initially trained, coached, and ultimately retained.

---

[1] *The Universal Sales Management Truths*, 2002, by Bill Brooks, Greensboro, NC: GamePlan Press.

2. Invest your time where it counts—with your highest performing or highest potential salespeople.

3. You can't manage or lead a sales team from behind a desk.

4. The greatest sales managers are the greatest identifiers and recruiters of top talent.

5. You can't lead where you won't go any more than you can teach what you don't know.

6. Hire salespeople with caution, launch them with clarity, and eliminate poor ones with great dispatch.

7. Pay plans are essential to sales success and ultimately determine how much of what gets sold.

8. Turnover in a salesforce is normal and to be expected. No turnover is bad and too high a turnover is even worse.

9. Don't allow digital tools or data gathering for other departments to dominate a sales team's life and stifle its creativity.

10. You can't motivate salespeople; you can only create an environment wherein they motivate themselves.

11. No salesperson will ever reach to any level of meaningful performance if expectations are not clearly established, communicated, and verified for his or her acceptance and understanding.

12. Performance counts in sales. However, accountability really pays.

13. A great salesperson who is poorly managed is no better than a poor salesperson managed well.

14. Effective sales managers are scouting for talented salespeople even if their roster is full.

15. Top salespeople consistently sell high volume at high margin.

16. A good interview is like a good sale: The candidate does most of the talking.

17. Don't hire salespeople until you observe them in social situations.

18. Effective sales managers have a lead management system in place.

19. A sales team will never perform any better than the way it is led and managed.

20. The three components of effective sales management are leadership, supervision, and management.

21. The best form of leadership for sales managers is to lead by example. The weakest is to lead by position.

22. Allowing too many sales contests to be run can be counter-productive. The result will be having too few winners and too many losers.

23. Poor sales managers create a situation where salespeople compete against other salespeople. Great sales managers allow salespeople to compete against their own previous best.

24. You can observe a salesperson's real effectiveness only in the field. You cannot do it through reports, statistics, or even through simply tracking results.

25. In-process evaluation is far superior to end-result evaluation. If you wait to judge sales performance solely on results, it's too late.

26. The best sales managers are inspiring.

27. Never miss an opportunity to coach, train, correct, observe, praise, provide feedback, or course-correct a salesperson's performance.

28. Effective sales management means a high prospect to customer closing ratio and an enthusiastic, well-paid sales team.

29. Sales management means just that—part sales and part management. However, they're not equal parts. Sales managers are managers first.

30. Great salespeople don't always make great sales managers.

31. Effective sales managers are systematic thinkers who know how to implement street-smart, practical, and usable strategies with their sales teams.

32. Powerful sales managers know it's not always what you say that is important. What is important is how you say it.

33. You get consistent results from salespeople by holding them accountable for their own goals, actions, activities, and results.

34. Sales managers who are doing their jobs understand the day-to-day problems salespeople face and develop processes and systems to reduce or eliminate them.

35. Effective sales management means helping salespeople with difficult sales and customer problems.

36. Successful sales managers want their salespeople to look good at every possible opportunity.

37. Knowing how to help salespeople manage their time and maximize the potential of their territory is a characteristic of the best sales managers.

38. Effective sales managers minimize the amount of busy work that is required from their sales team.

39. Leadership is inspiring salespeople to achieve peak performance.

40. Management is the establishment of standards and procedures whereas supervision is holding salespeople accountable for meeting those standards. Both are essential for good sales management.

41. Sales managers who are most effective are not afraid to show their own humanity and weaknesses.

42. Great sales managers know where to draw the line between being too friendly and too distant. Knowing where that line is often determines the difference between greatness and mediocrity.

43. Good sales managers empower their sales teams to believe that they are better than they really are. And then they coach them to legitimately be that good.

44. Teaching occurs in the classroom. Coaching occurs in the field. You need to do both to get salespeople to maximize their capacities.

45. Allowing salespeople to establish their own sales goals is powerful and productive. Salespeople then take ownership for achieving what they themselves have committed to doing.

46. Sales managers have to spend time with salespeople to help them implement strategies and tactics. They can't be left on their own to do it.

47. A salesperson who receives no feedback is like a directionless ship. It has no idea where it has been, where it is going, or how to get there.

48. A great sales manager is like a great coach. You must place the right player in the right place at the right time.

49. Sales managers must have the responsibility to perform and the authority to act and then be willing to be held accountable for their own actions and results.

50. It is far easier to demotivate than it is to motivate. Powerful sales managers are always conscious of what they say and how it is interpreted.

51. Salespeople must be given the authority to negotiate price, terms, and conditions to the level that is commensurate with their experience and capabilities.

52. Sales managers who are self-confident allow salespeople to observe them selling and then solicit feedback from the salespeople who watch them sell.

53. If you want to become extremely proficient at something, teach it. That includes sales.

54. The most powerful thing a sales manager can do is to go on joint calls and then conduct curbside coaching sessions with salespeople.

55. Never pass up an opportunity to praise a salesperson in front of other salespeople, managers, customers, prospects, or the salesperson's family.

56. Sales managers who are on top of their game never stop studying sales, salespeople, or the sales profession.

57. Leading a group of salespeople is like no other management position in the world. Salespeople are more difficult, demanding, and free spirited than any other group. Yet, they are also more appreciative and genuine.

58. Effective sales managers never act on hearsay or rumor. Instead, they research the facts and act on them in a timely manner.

59. Treat all salespeople fairly, but don't treat them all the same. Each one is unique. Treat them that way.

60. Salespeople learn from what they experience and do, not just from what they hear.

61. Sales flies on the wings of words. Powerful sales managers ensure that each sales team member can use the words that reflect the philosophy and positioning of the organization and its products and services.

62. Sales managers should serve as the link between sales and marketing departments and must ensure that both departments understand and communicate with each other.

63. Salespeople learn as much from mistakes as they do from successes. Probably more. Turn defeats into opportunities to coach, mentor, and teach.

64. Salespeople are looking for powerful role models. One of those role models should be their sales manager.

65. Salespeople expect and deserve timely feedback. That's why schedules and time lines are essential and must always be met.

66. Never postpone, cancel, or overlook a scheduled training session, performance review, appraisal, or scheduled feedback session with a salesperson.

67. Respected sales managers are punctual and timely with all promised documents, reports, and related items for salespeople.

68. Effective sales managers never take credit for ideas that were originally developed by members of their sales team.

69. Good sales managers never say, "Do it because I said so." Instead, they give good reasons and a solid rationale behind each of their directives.

70. Salespeople need to know the *why* behind every *how*.

71. Sales managers who get the best from their sales team know that sales education and training never stops for them or their sales team.

72. Productive sales managers never say or do anything in haste. They stop to think about the ramifications of their words and acts before saying or doing anything.

73. Respected sales managers are people of their word. They never make a promise or commitment to a salesperson that they can't keep.

74. Good sales managers are marketplace, product, and service experts. They possess unique understanding and wisdom related to how to sell their product or service and the unique value it brings to customers.

75. Marketplace know-how and an in-depth understanding of competitors, suppliers, associations, trade organizations, and all their constituencies are essential for good sales management.

76. Successful sales managers work on their sales team and not in them. There is a big difference.

77. Sales managers who build great sales teams manage their own time well so that they always have time to invest with each team member.

78. Powerful sales managers conduct regular sales meetings and always invest time in those meetings for communication, product knowledge enhancement, and sales skills training for salespeople.

79. Sales managers who understand that the last thing to meddle with is a salesperson's income tend to have more productive salespeople.

80. Sales managers need to understand that there has never been a compensation plan developed anywhere, by anyone or any organization that has made every salesperson happy.

81. Salespeople need to be compensated for things over which they have control (sales)—not for things over which they have no control (net profit).

82. Never energize incompetence. Motivation without education or meaningful skill development yields nothing but frustration.

83. Sales managers need to understand that communication can be your greatest tool. It can also be your worst enemy. So manage it carefully.

84. Sales managers who succeed understand the power of high expectations and constant feedback to salespeople concerning those expectations.

85. The best sales managers know the power of appropriate attire and ensure that both they and their salespeople always dress accordingly.

86. Great sales managers know that the best way around a problem, dilemma, difficulty, or challenge is often to head straight through it.

87. Good sales managers know that education is better than ignorance regardless of price.

88. Powerful sales managers don't major in minors. They do the right things more often.

89. The best sales managers know how important fun, humor, and a playful attitude are to their salespeople.

90. Great sales managers deal with fact and performance instead of rumor, bias, or stereotypes.

91. A nonresponsive sales manager quickly loses the respect of salespeople. Projects, ideas, feedback, promises, solicited input, and details never seem to get implemented. Instead, they go into a black hole. Avoid this at all costs.

92. Successful sales managers work harder than the salespeople who report to them. Becoming a sales manager doesn't mean less work. It means more.

93. Don't allow forms, reports, data, checklists, or information gathering to stifle a sales team's creativity.

94. The most effective sales managers know the progress and status of every prospect and customer each salesperson is working with on a daily basis.

95. Good sales managers expect salespeople to be able to explain what they do and how they do it. They understand that if salespeople cannot explain something, they can't do it.

96. Intellectual understanding of sales is critical. However, outstanding sales managers know that the best salespeople have a deep and passionate understanding of selling that is far deeper than merely an intellectual grasp of it.

97. Great sales managers ensure their salespeople have a linked, sequential sales process to follow and then ensure that salespeople follow it.

98. The best sales managers know that what motivates them may not motivate each individual salesperson.

99. Sales managers who succeed are consistent in the way they respond to issues, problems, and concerns. Salespeople don't like or need volatility. They covet predictability.

100. Fantastic sales managers are like fantastic coaches. They can spot talent, recruit the right people, coach, train, and retain champions. And they do it year after year.

101. Superstar sales managers invest their time with responsive people. They don't waste valuable time with people who refuse to respond.

Bonus

Sales managers who succeed know how to celebrate success, learn from failures, and sustain positive, productive momentum with the right people.

Smart companies guarantee that the salespeople who are part of their organization sell well enough to become great salespeople. They empower them with knowledge, skills, and support. They also ensure that their salespeople are totally grounded in solid twenty-first century smart selling strategies and philosophy. These organizations strive to drive the 101 Universal Sales Truths to their sales teams. Like the sales management truths, we list first those discussed earlier in this book. However, just like the previous list, there are many others that are just as valuable as well:

101 Universal Sales Truths[2]

1. Prospects pay attention to people they believe have something important to say to them.

2. People buy for their own reasons, not for yours or mine.

3. People do not want to be sold, but they do want to buy.

[2] *The Universal Sales Management Truths*, 2002, by Bill Brooks, Greensboro, NC: GamePlan Press.

4. When a salesperson and a customer get locked into a war of the wills, the salesperson always loses.

5. Buying is basically an emotional response no matter what you're selling.

6. Being the sort of salesperson people enjoy doing business with is an invaluable asset.

7. If you don't close sales, you won't make a living as a salesperson.

8. Prospects must believe you before they'll buy from you. And that's much tougher to do than you think.

9. You can convince others only of what you yourself believe.

10. The more you believe in yourself, the easier it is to get others to believe what you say.

11. A strong, positive self-concept is the most valuable personal attribute any salesperson can have.

12. When you believe, you can make others believe. When you don't, no one else will, either.

13. Your customer will never believe in the value of your product or service any more strongly than you do.

14. The seller determines the cost of its product or service, but only the buyer can determine its true value.

15. People pay much more attention to what you are than to what you say.

16. Show people what they *need* most in a way they *want* to see it, and they will move heaven and earth to get it.

17. People are always too busy to waste time doing anything they don't really want to do.

18. It is always easier to sell to a prospect's perceived need than to create need in the prospect's mind.

19. All values are equal until someone points out the difference.

20. The secret to successful selling is not in the selling at all. Instead, it is in the accurate, consistent science of prospecting.

21. The vital part of any sale is seldom the close but what takes place before the sales interview even begins.

22. The better job of finding qualified prospects you do, the higher your closing average will be.

23. The most productive sentence in any salesperson's vocabulary always ends with a question mark.

24. Treat prospecting as the lifeblood of your sales career because it is.

25. You never know when your prospect's motivation to buy will suddenly and dramatically escalate.

26. The only certain way to ensure you, your organization, or product are thought of first is through frequent, repetitious contact.

27. Constantly search for a person who can give you a referral for each prospect or . . . better yet . . . make the initial contact for you.

28. Unless you get people to lower their mental/emotional defenses and let you in, eliminate tension and establish trust, build rapport, and start a successful sales dialogue, you cannot move forward to make the sale.

29. The best way to serve your own interest is to put the needs and desires of your customer first.

30. To deliver value to the prospect, you must see yourself primarily as a value resource for the prospect.

31. To be a value resource for the prospect, you must first discover what your prospect perceives as value.

32. Never interrupt a prospect. However, you need to be interruptible.

33. Get your whole body involved in listening and show that you are paying attention. Look the person squarely in the eye and use facial expressions and gestures to show that you hear and understand what's being said.

34. All values are considered equal in the absence of a values interpreter.

35. The fatal flaw in selling occurs when you are so focused on what you want to happen that you lose sight of what the prospect wants to happen.

36. To a prospect, any price is too high until he or she understands the value of your product or service.

37. Always tailor your presentation to the prospect's *needs* and *wants* . . . not to yours.

38. All sales degenerate into a struggle over price in the absence of a value interpreter.

39. Avoid making price an issue yourself.

40. All values are considered equal until someone points out the difference.

41. What people believe strongly enough, they act on.

42. Never make a claim you can't back up with facts.

43. It makes little difference what you believe to be true unless you can prove it to your prospect.

44. Prospects expect salespeople to make claims for what they are selling, but they are impressed when someone else makes or endorses those claims.

45. As trust in you and confidence in the value of what you are offering rises, fear of buying disappears.

46. Always assure buyers of the wisdom of their choices.

47. Concentrate on results, not on activities.

48. True, long-lasting enthusiasm is born on the inside.

49. Enthusiasm grows when you focus on solutions and opportunities instead of problems and circumstances.

50. Most of the things that can go wrong in sales happen when a salesperson's mouth is open.

51. There are four areas where you can focus: self, company, product, or customer. If you focus on the first three, your customer is outnumbered three to one.

52. To be a top sales professional enjoying long-range success, you must be an intelligent investor of your time, talent, resources, and energies.

53. Marketing strategy is what gets you to the customer's door in the best possible light. Sales strategy is what you do when you are inside.

54. You may have to take whatever comes your way in life, but you have to go after what you want to be a sales winner.

55. Price alone is rarely a key factor in buying decisions. Instead, the key factor in any buying decision is the perceived value to be gained by the buyer.

56. In a crowded marketplace, all other things being equal, the one with the most information who knows how to use it wins.

57. Let your questions do the selling for you.

58. Listen people into buying instead of talking your way out of the sale.

59. Get your prospects to openly share how they feel about what they have seen and heard so you will always know where you stand.

60. Your attitude toward sales as a profession determines your selling actions.

61. When selling, connect with your own deepest values and never settle to invest a moment in anything less.

62. Salespeople who do only what they feel like doing today are bound to spend the rest of their lives unable to do what they really feel like doing.

63. Trust produces an open mind, and mistrust produces a closed mind. If you gain trust, the decision maker says:

"Tell me how you can satisfy my *needs*" (open mind). If you achieve mistrust, the decision maker says: "You can't satisfy my *needs*" (closed mind).

64. You have to address the decision maker's emotions before you address his or her intellect. A hungry stomach cannot hear.

65. When the average decision maker doesn't buy, he or she remembers fewer than 10 words spoken verbatim by the salesperson during the presentation.

66. The average decision maker spends only between 9 and 20 seconds reviewing written sales materials. The average decision maker spends only between 4 and 11 seconds reviewing a print ad.

67. The typical objection is the rational justification for an emotional decision that was made long before the objection is expressed.

68. An objection is almost always an indication that the decision maker has a closed mind. Therefore, the objection usually has nothing to do with what caused the emotional resistance.

69. Most decision makers are more interested in the person they're buying from than in the thing they're buying.

70. Never position yourself, your organization, or what you're selling on the basis of a feature or a benefit.

71. Successful selling amounts to making the decision maker feel good and being in the room when he or she does feel good.

72. More than 80 percent of all salespeople talk more than is necessary to secure a sale.

73. Goals define the way you shape your own life.

74. The two main ingredients for enthusiasm are being captivated by an ideal and having a deep conviction that you can achieve it.

75. Compete against the achievement of your sales objectives, not against the successes of others or their expectations of you.

76. Dwell on your past sales successes. View past failures only as lessons learned.

77. A selling career is a continuous series of opportunities. The way we handle those opportunities is the way we handle our career.

78. Associate with positive, successful people and you will be more positive and successful.

79. The secret to selling is to be in front of qualified prospects when they're ready to buy, not when you need to make a sale.

80. Take an organized approach to prospecting . . . but never at the expense of activity.

81. Never violate the formal structure of an organization . . . but master an understanding of the informal.

82. You have only a matter of seconds to establish your credibility and convince a prospect that time spent with you will be valuable.

83. Without trust, you can sell only price. With trust you can sell value.

84. Focus on what prospects are saying—not what they're going to say or what you're going to say.

85. When presenting price, always avoid cushioning statements such as: "Here we go . . .," "Are you ready for this?" or "Are you sitting down?"

86. Never use set-up statements such as: "Tell me where we need to be . . .," "The list price is . . .," or "I want your business so . . ."

87. Always ensure that value exceeds price; then, and only then, present your price as related strictly to value.

88. Finalizing agreement and closing sales is a consequence of what has happened early in the sale rather than something the sale builds toward.

89. Selling is a science that, when practiced correctly, can become an art.

90. The fear of loss is as powerful as the joy of gain.

91. The jump from character (what you are) to reputation (what people think you are) is much smaller than many salespeople would like to believe.

92. Once you discover what your prospect perceives his or her most pressing need, build your whole presentation around that need.

93. Value-based salespeople always concern themselves first and foremost with how the prospect perceives his or her needs.

94. Uncover your prospects' needs as they perceive them, and then enable them to meet those needs through what you are selling.

95. Canned sales presentations are insulting to today's educated and alert consumers, many of whom are professional buyers.

96. Lack of qualified prospects is the greatest single cause of failure among salespeople. Prospecting is the toughest part of selling.

97. Good prospecting is a matter of developing a solid game plan that works well for you and following that game plan to the letter.

98. There is a vast difference between self-centeredness and serving your own best interest.

99. If all you want to talk about is yourself—your interests, products, features, or organization—don't be surprised if you encounter strong sales resistance from the outset.

100. What allows salespeople to be differentiated from a vending machine is that salespeople have an opportunity to meet the widely varied and specific needs of each customer they serve.

101. Listening is a skill that can be learned and continuously improved, but most of us have never been trained to listen. For example, which do we do most during the day: talk or listen?

Bonus

A *pitch* is what is delivered from the pitcher's mound to home plate. Sales professionals *don't pitch*; they make professional sales presentations.

Organizational and
Salesforce Audit

This chapter contains 10 sets of audits, one for each of the first 10 chapters of this book. There are a total of 20 audits. There are 10 that can be completed by sales executives or managers relative to each of the 10 chapters and another 10 that salespeople can complete by registering their opinions on the same issues. In all, there are 228 questions whose answers can be analyzed, compared, and reviewed.

The purpose of these audits is to enable entire sales organizations to analyze themselves by allowing sales executives or managers to register their opinions on their own products and for salespeople to do the same. There is little doubt that self-discovery and realistic self-appraisal is key to forging a successful and profitable sales organization. These audits can be a powerful, productive first step in that direction.

Chapter 1 Audit—Sales Management

	Yes	No	Not Sure	N/A
1. Are we teaching up-to-date, current sales methods to our salespeople?	☐	☐	☐	☐
2. Are we teaching our salespeople to do the right, relevant things?	☐	☐	☐	☐
3. Do we teach proper prospecting, precall planning, and positioning to our salespeople?	☐	☐	☐	☐
4. Are we doing all in our power to differentiate our product offerings?	☐	☐	☐	☐
5. Do we have bundles and varied levels of offerings?	☐	☐	☐	☐
6. Do we provide our salespeople up-to-the-minute tools and sales aids?	☐	☐	☐	☐
7. Do we adequately train salespeople how to sell new products as they roll out?	☐	☐	☐	☐
8. Are we working to reduce the amount of cold calling that is required of our salespeople?	☐	☐	☐	☐
9. Do we really think through our promotion policy concerning selection of the most effective sales management candidates?	☐	☐	☐	☐
10. If we have sales automation software, have we gotten sufficient input from salespeople about its selection, design, or requirements?	☐	☐	☐	☐
11. Have we sufficiently stressed the role that margin plays in our sales effort?	☐	☐	☐	☐
12. Do we have a pay plan based on (1) margin, (2) volume, and (3) consistency?	☐	☐	☐	☐
13. Do we sufficiently reward sales success?	☐	☐	☐	☐
14. Do we clearly define sales success?	☐	☐	☐	☐

Chapter 1 Audit—Sales

	Yes	No	Not Sure	N/A
1. Am I being taught up-to-date, current sales methods?	☐	☐	☐	☐
2. Am I receiving adequate sales skills training?	☐	☐	☐	☐
3. Do I know how to position myself, the organization, and the products?	☐	☐	☐	☐
4. Do I have a solid, consistent set of prospecting tools?	☐	☐	☐	☐
5. Do I have a complete precall planning checklist?	☐	☐	☐	☐
6. Do I know how to differentiate my products or services from the competition?	☐	☐	☐	☐
7. Do I have fresh, up-to-date sales tools and sales aids?	☐	☐	☐	☐
8. Am I adequately trained to sell new products or services before they are introduced?	☐	☐	☐	☐
9. Has my organization provided me the tools to move beyond cold calling to get new prospects?	☐	☐	☐	☐
10. Do I feel that I receive the level of sales management support and field coaching I need?	☐	☐	☐	☐
11. Am I expected to spend minimal time inputting data, learning, or mastering a salesforce automation or customer relationship management system?	☐	☐	☐	☐
12. Am I rewarded in any way for achieving superior margin on my sales?	☐	☐	☐	☐
13. Do I know exactly how I am rewarded for margin, volume, and/or consistency in sales?	☐	☐	☐	☐
14. Do I know what defines successful sales performance in my organization?	☐	☐	☐	☐

Chapter 2 Audit—Sales Management

	Yes	No	Not Sure	N/A
1. Do we have a formal, structured training program for sales managers?	☐	☐	☐	☐
2. Do we have clear expectations, in writing, that explain exactly what sales managers are expected to do on a day-to-day basis?	☐	☐	☐	☐
3. Do we have a performance management system in place that allows us to evaluate sales managers' performance against exact standards?	☐	☐	☐	☐
4. Is our salesforce recruitment, selection, and hiring process relevant, up-to-date, and effective?	☐	☐	☐	☐
5. Are our sales managers strong, effective leaders?	☐	☐	☐	☐
6. Do we have a strong system in place for launching new salespeople with great clarity and with the clear expectations held for them?	☐	☐	☐	☐
7. Does our pay plan reward the things that should be rewarded?	☐	☐	☐	☐
8. Do we have an acceptable level of turnover on our sales team?	☐	☐	☐	☐
9. Do we have a pay plan that rewards performance and eliminates stagnation?	☐	☐	☐	☐
10. Do we know, with exact precision, how to manage and motivate each salesperson individually?	☐	☐	☐	☐
11. Do our salespeople know the exact expectations that we hold for them on an ongoing basis?	☐	☐	☐	☐
12. Do we hold both our sales management and sales teams accountable for their actions in measurable ways?	☐	☐	☐	☐
13. Do our sales managers spend enough time in the field with salespeople?	☐	☐	☐	☐
14. Do our sales managers spend quality time coaching salespeople?	☐	☐	☐	☐
15. Do our sales managers have strong product knowledge and selling skills themselves?	☐	☐	☐	☐

Chapter 2 Audit—Sales

	Yes	No	Not Sure	N/A
1. Do I feel that my sales manager has been adequately trained to do his or her job?	☐	☐	☐	☐
2. Do I know exactly what my sales manager is expected to provide to me in terms of support and assistance?	☐	☐	☐	☐
3. Do I feel that my sales manager's performance is evaluated as it should be?	☐	☐	☐	☐
4. Do I feel that our process for selecting new salespeople will help us to continue to hire the best?	☐	☐	☐	☐
5. Do I consider my sales manager to be an effective, strong leader who advocates strongly for me?	☐	☐	☐	☐
6. Does our organization launch new salespeople with great clarity and an accurate understanding of the exact expectations held for them?	☐	☐	☐	☐
7. Does my pay plan reward superior performance?	☐	☐	☐	☐
8. Do we have methods to eliminate turnover of salespeople in our organization?	☐	☐	☐	☐
9. Does our pay plan eliminate a sense of complacency and a sense of entitlement on the part of salespeople?	☐	☐	☐	☐
10. Does my sales manager know how to manage, communicate with, and motivate me?	☐	☐	☐	☐
11. Do I know exactly what my sales manager expects me to do in the correct ways?	☐	☐	☐	☐
12. Am I held accountable for daily actions and results?	☐	☐	☐	☐
13. Do I feel that my sales manager spends sufficient time with me in the field?	☐	☐	☐	☐
14. Do I receive real-time, meaningful coaching from my sales manager?	☐	☐	☐	☐
15. Do I believe my sales manager has strong product knowledge and personal selling skills?	☐	☐	☐	☐

Chapter 3 Audit—Sales Management

	Yes	No	Not Sure	N/A
1. Do we have a high enough applicant-to-hiree ratio?	☐	☐	☐	☐
2. Have we determined the turnover cost for each salesperson we lose?	☐	☐	☐	☐
3. Do we know all of the problems that turnover of salespeople costs us?	☐	☐	☐	☐
4. Do we have a process in place to match the applicant's interests and values to what the job rewards?	☐	☐	☐	☐
5. Do we have a method to benchmark each unique sales job and assess an applicant against the job?	☐	☐	☐	☐
6. Do we have a method to curtail the hiring of applicants from only our industry?	☐	☐	☐	☐
7. Do we have a method to objectively determine applicants' selling skills before hiring them?	☐	☐	☐	☐
8. Do we have a method to determine each applicant's personal skills?	☐	☐	☐	☐
9. Do we take adequate time to hire salespeople?	☐	☐	☐	☐
10. Do we feel that we hire only the best applicants?	☐	☐	☐	☐

Chapter 3 Audit—Sales

	Yes	No	Not Sure	N/A
1. Was the process for hiring me in this sales position rigorous enough?	☐	☐	☐	☐
2. Do I know exactly what my sales position expects and requires of me?	☐	☐	☐	☐
3. Do I feel that I am 100 percent compatible with the expectations of my job?	☐	☐	☐	☐
4. Does my current sales job reward me with the day-to-day psychic rewards that keep me committed?	☐	☐	☐	☐
5. Do we have a balance of salespeople with backgrounds from both inside the industry and outside our industry?	☐	☐	☐	☐
6. Were my actual selling skills assessed in any way before I was hired for this job?	☐	☐	☐	☐
7. Do I feel that our organization attracts and hires only the best?	☐	☐	☐	☐
8. Do I feel that the bar is always being raised when new salespeople are hired?	☐	☐	☐	☐
9. Do I feel that all applicants are screened as thoroughly as they should be before being hired?	☐	☐	☐	☐

Chapter 4 Audit—Sales Management

	Yes	No	Not Sure	N/A
1. Have we sufficiently addressed the role that leadership plays in sales management?	☐	☐	☐	☐
2. Are we looking at *all* of the variables that go into successful sales management?	☐	☐	☐	☐
3. Do we avoid being haphazard in our hiring practices?	☐	☐	☐	☐
4. Do we avoid the practice of promoting strong sales performers into sales management roles?	☐	☐	☐	☐
5. Do we avoid subscribing to the belief that superior sales skills automatically translate into superior sales management skills?	☐	☐	☐	☐
6. Do we avoid promoting people into sales management according to the assumption that unless someone has been the number one salesperson, the sales team will not respect or follow that person?	☐	☐	☐	☐
7. Do we stress that the attributes associated with sales management differ from the attributes associated with sales?	☐	☐	☐	☐
8. Are our sales management hiring practices as rigorous as our sales hiring practices?	☐	☐	☐	☐
9. Are we looking inside and outside our organization when hiring sales managers?	☐	☐	☐	☐
10. When promoting sales managers from within, do we help newly promoted sales managers adjust from being part of the team to being a leader of the team?	☐	☐	☐	☐
11. Do we select the most qualified sales managers regardless of where we find them?	☐	☐	☐	☐
12. Do we set clear standards and expectations for the sales team?	☐	☐	☐	☐
13. Do we provide feedback against those standards and expectations?	☐	☐	☐	☐

Chapter 4 Audit—Sales Management *(Continued)*

	Yes	No	Not Sure	N/A
14. Do we maintain tight metrics for the expectations placed on salespeople?	☐	☐	☐	☐
15. Is the feedback we give honest, sincere, consistent, and as objective as possible?	☐	☐	☐	☐
16. Do we make teaching and coaching the top priority?	☐	☐	☐	☐

Chapter 4 Audit—Sales

	Yes	No	Not Sure	N/A
1. Is my sales manager concerned with the role that leadership plays in his or her position?	☐	☐	☐	☐
2. Does my sales manager look at all of the variables associated with the successful execution of the sales position?	☐	☐	☐	☐
3. Does sales management avoid being haphazard in its hiring practices?	☐	☐	☐	☐
4. Is sales management avoiding the promotion of salespeople into sales management roles based solely on sales performance?	☐	☐	☐	☐
5. Does sales management stress that the attributes associated with sales management differ from the attributes associated with sales?	☐	☐	☐	☐
6. Are sales management hiring practices as rigorous as sales hiring practices?	☐	☐	☐	☐
7. Are we looking inside and outside our organization when hiring sales managers?	☐	☐	☐	☐
8. When promoting sales managers from within, does my organization help newly promoted sales managers adjust from being part of the team to being a leader of the team?	☐	☐	☐	☐
9. Does sales management select the most qualified sales managers regardless of where they're found?	☐	☐	☐	☐
10. Does my sales manager set clear standards and expectations for me?	☐	☐	☐	☐
11. Does my sales manager provide feedback against those standards and expectations?	☐	☐	☐	☐
12. Does my sales manager maintain tight metrics for the expectations placed on me?	☐	☐	☐	☐
13. Is the feedback I'm given honest, sincere, consistent, and as objective as possible?	☐	☐	☐	☐
14. Does my sales manager make teaching and coaching the top priority?	☐	☐	☐	☐

Chapter 5 Audit—Sales Management

	Yes	No	Not Sure	N/A
1. Do our sales managers have both the responsibility and authority to do their jobs?	☐	☐	☐	☐
2. Do we have an aggressive recruitment program in place to attract consistently strong salespeople?	☐	☐	☐	☐
3. Do we have a sales management system in place that all sales managers implement and follow regularly?	☐	☐	☐	☐
4. Do we have adequate, ongoing training that makes our organization a learning leader?	☐	☐	☐	☐
5. Do we provide regular, consistent sales training for salespeople?	☐	☐	☐	☐
6. Do our sales managers spend enough time in the field coaching salespeople?	☐	☐	☐	☐
7. Do our salespeople receive regular and consistent feedback about their performance?	☐	☐	☐	☐
8. Do we have a method in place for easily tracking a salesperson's day-to-day activities?	☐	☐	☐	☐
9. Do we have a system for short-term, measurable accountability of salespeople other than reviewing sales results?	☐	☐	☐	☐
10. Do we have a quota, target, or goal-setting process that allows salespeople to establish their own sales targets?	☐	☐	☐	☐

Chapter 5 Audit—Sales

	Yes	No	Not Sure	N/A
1. Do I feel that my sales manager has enough legitimate authority to do his or her job?	☐	☐	☐	☐
2. Do I feel that we attract the best possible candidates for sales positions?	☐	☐	☐	☐
3. Is there is a consistent process to the way I am managed?	☐	☐	☐	☐
4. Does this organization provide balanced, ongoing training for salespeople?	☐	☐	☐	☐
5. Does my sales manager spend enough time in the field with me?	☐	☐	☐	☐
6. Is the time that my manager spends with me productive and valuable?	☐	☐	☐	☐
7. Do I have a simple, easy-to-use method for tracking the day-to-day activities?	☐	☐	☐	☐
8. Do I know what day-to-day activities I am supposed to be doing?	☐	☐	☐	☐
9. Do I feel that I'm held accountable for things other than sales results?	☐	☐	☐	☐
10. Do I have any input into sales quotas, targets, or goals?	☐	☐	☐	☐

Chapter 6 Audit—Sales Management

	Yes	No	Not Sure	N/A
1. Do we have an adequate orientation program for new salespeople?	☐	☐	☐	☐
2. Do salespeople receive in-depth information about the organization's history, vision, mission, and goals?	☐	☐	☐	☐
3. Do salespeople receive formal information about our marketplace and products?	☐	☐	☐	☐
4. Have we avoided the tendency to rely too much on current, experienced salespeople to pass on valuable knowledge to new salespeople?	☐	☐	☐	☐
5. Do we teach our salespeople how to position themselves as business experts rather than salespeople?	☐	☐	☐	☐
6. Do our salespeople listen enough?	☐	☐	☐	☐
7. Do we teach our salespeople how to sell value?	☐	☐	☐	☐
8. Do we have a value proposition that starts and ends with the customer?	☐	☐	☐	☐
9. Do our salespeople know the difference between the formal and informal structure of their prospect's organization?	☐	☐	☐	☐
10. Do we teach our salespeople exactly when and how to close sales?	☐	☐	☐	☐
11. Do we have a system to ensure that our salespeople truly believe in our products and services?	☐	☐	☐	☐
12. Do we stress that it is the quality of the contacts that our salespeople make that is important?	☐	☐	☐	☐
13. Do we work hard enough to ensure that our salespeople have true mastery of selling skills, product knowledge, personal skills, and marketplace expertise?	☐	☐	☐	☐

Chapter 6 Audit—Sales

	Yes	No	Not Sure	N/A
1. Do I believe that I and other salespeople received a strong orientation to the history, background, and expectations of this organization?	☐	☐	☐	☐
2. Do I believe that I and other salespeople received enough information about the mission, direction, and traditions of this organization when first hired?	☐	☐	☐	☐
3. Do I believe that other salespeople and I received sufficient marketplace and product information early in our employment cycle?	☐	☐	☐	☐
4. Do I believe that too much reliance is placed on existing salespeople helping new salespeople to learn the ropes of the job?	☐	☐	☐	☐
5. Have I been taught how to position myself as anything other than a salesperson?	☐	☐	☐	☐
6. Have I been taught how to listen?	☐	☐	☐	☐
7. Do I know exactly how to sell value rather than price?	☐	☐	☐	☐
8. Do I know what real, true customer focus is?	☐	☐	☐	☐
9. Do I know the difference between a prospect's formal and informal structure?	☐	☐	☐	☐
10. Have I been taught exactly when and how to close sales?	☐	☐	☐	☐
11. Do I believe, with no doubt whatsoever, that the products I sell are worth more than what we ask prospects to pay for them?	☐	☐	☐	☐
12. Am I required to complete a prescribed number of activities daily (phone calls, visits, etc.) only with qualified prospects?	☐	☐	☐	☐
13. Do I feel that I have the opportunity to gain total mastery of selling skills, product knowledge, personal skills, and marketplace expertise?	☐	☐	☐	☐

Chapter 7 Audit—Sales Management

	Yes	No	Not Sure	N/A
1. Do we have a dominant culture in our organization?	☐	☐	☐	☐
2. Is our sales department viewed as friendly by internal constituencies?	☐	☐	☐	☐
3. Is our sales department profitable?	☐	☐	☐	☐
4. Does our organization believe it could not thrive without the sales department?	☐	☐	☐	☐
5. Is the sales department supported by key executives?	☐	☐	☐	☐
6. Do the sales department standards exceed those of other departments?	☐	☐	☐	☐
7. Do all members of the sales team interface well with other departments?	☐	☐	☐	☐
8. Does the sales department bring great value to the organization?	☐	☐	☐	☐
9. Do members of the salesforce mesh well with other departments?	☐	☐	☐	☐
10. Is the salesforce made up of competent, capable high performers?	☐	☐	☐	☐
11. Does our salesforce have clear, measurable expectations other than sales quotas?	☐	☐	☐	☐
12. Does our sales team receive regular development reviews and improvement plans to follow?	☐	☐	☐	☐

Chapter 7 Audit—Sales

	Yes	No	Not Sure	N/A
1. Do I know what defines our company (are we a sales, marketing, distribution, service, operations, administrative, or research and development organization)?	☐	☐	☐	☐
2. Is the sales department viewed favorably by other departments?	☐	☐	☐	☐
3. Do I know if the sales department is profitable?	☐	☐	☐	☐
4. Does our organization believe it needs a sales department?	☐	☐	☐	☐
5. Does the sales department have the support it needs for senior-level executives?	☐	☐	☐	☐
6. Do the standards in the sales department exceed those of other departments?	☐	☐	☐	☐
7. Do all members of the sales department show respect and appreciation for other departments?	☐	☐	☐	☐
8. Do I feel that the sales department brings great value to the organization?	☐	☐	☐	☐
9. Do all members of the sales department interact favorably with people in other departments?	☐	☐	☐	☐
10. Do I believe that all members of the sales department are totally capable of superior performance?	☐	☐	☐	☐
11. Do I have clear, measurable expectations for things other than achieving a sales target?	☐	☐	☐	☐
12. Do I receive regular reviews and improvement plans?	☐	☐	☐	☐

Chapter 8 Audit—Sales Management

	Yes	No	Not Sure	N/A
1. Does our organization measure the right activities that salespeople should be doing?	☐	☐	☐	☐
2. Do we make salespeople answerable enough for their own daily actions?	☐	☐	☐	☐
3. Do we give our salespeople clear levels of responsibility?	☐	☐	☐	☐
4. Do we give our salespeople clear levels of authority?	☐	☐	☐	☐
5. Do the levels of responsibility and authority match?	☐	☐	☐	☐
6. Do we reward our salespeople for the right things?	☐	☐	☐	☐
7. Does our pay plan drive achievement?	☐	☐	☐	☐

Chapter 8 Audit—Sales

	Yes	No	Not Sure	N/A
1. Am I held accountable for doing the right things in my job?	☐	☐	☐	☐
2. Am I held answerable enough for my own daily actions?	☐	☐	☐	☐
3. Do I understand the level of responsibility I have been given?	☐	☐	☐	☐
4. Do I know how much authority I have been given?	☐	☐	☐	☐
5. Do I feel that the levels of responsibility and authority I have are equal?	☐	☐	☐	☐
6. Do I feel that our sales compensation plan rewards salespeople for the right things?	☐	☐	☐	☐
7. Do I believe that our plan rewards superior performance?	☐	☐	☐	☐

Chapter 9 Audit—Sales Management

	Yes	No	Not Sure	N/A
1. Are we ensuring that the marketing, sales, and service efforts are as integrated as possible?	☐	☐	☐	☐
2. Are our promises, our customers' expectations, and their experiences in alignment with one another?	☐	☐	☐	☐
3. Are we placing actual marketing tools and strategies into the hands of our sales and service departments that interface with prospects and customers while simultaneously expanding our marketing message?	☐	☐	☐	☐
4. Do we ensure our salespeople know exactly and precisely how our organization, products, and the salespeople themselves are positioned in the market?	☐	☐	☐	☐
5. Do we ensure that the sales, marketing, and service departments never operate in isolation?	☐	☐	☐	☐
6. Do we provide some form of minimal sales training for service and technical people?	☐	☐	☐	☐
7. Do we ensure that whenever someone in a service or technical support role is on a sales call with a salesperson, both are on the same page at the same time?	☐	☐	☐	☐
8. Do we place valuable and usable tools in the hands of salespeople that are an extension of our marketing message?	☐	☐	☐	☐
9. Do we send the same segue that was articulated between marketing and sales to the service department as well?	☐	☐	☐	☐
10. Do we hold our sales team accountable for exceeding the expectations held for the sales experience?	☐	☐	☐	☐
11. Have we sufficiently ensured that everyone who ever sees, talks with, associates with, or comes in contact with a prospect or customer understand exactly what the promise–expectation–experience chain is?	☐	☐	☐	☐

Chapter 9 Audit—Sales

	Yes	No	Not Sure	N/A
1. Are the marketing, sales, and service efforts as integrated as possible?	☐	☐	☐	☐
2. Are my promises, my customers' expectations, and their experiences in alignment with one another?	☐	☐	☐	☐
3. Do I have access to actual marketing tools and strategies that expand our marketing message?	☐	☐	☐	☐
4. Do I know exactly and precisely how my organization and I are positioned in the market?	☐	☐	☐	☐
5. Does my organization make sure that the sales, marketing, and service departments never operate in isolation?	☐	☐	☐	☐
6. Does my organization provide some form of minimal sales training for service and technical people?	☐	☐	☐	☐
7. Does my organization ensure that whenever someone in a service or technical support role is on a sales call with me, we are on the same page at the same time?	☐	☐	☐	☐
8. Am I held accountable for exceeding the expectations held by my prospects for the sales experience?	☐	☐	☐	☐

Chapter 10 Audit—Sales Management

	Yes	No	*Not Sure*	*N/A*
1. Are our product launches carefully planned significantly before new products are introduced to the field?	☐	☐	☐	☐
2. Do we field-test sales aids and sales tools before we use them in the field with new products?	☐	☐	☐	☐
3. Do we invest adequate time and effort training salespeople on new products?	☐	☐	☐	☐
4. Are we careful not to introduce too many new products too soon?	☐	☐	☐	☐
5. Do we adequately work out all the potential bugs before introducing new products?	☐	☐	☐	☐
6. Do we provide salespeople with all the knowledge they need about the competition before we roll out a new product?	☐	☐	☐	☐
7. Do we solicit feedback from the field about prospect or customer response to new products?	☐	☐	☐	☐
8. Do we take action in a timely manner based on what the field tells us?	☐	☐	☐	☐
9. Do we update training and tools as we get data from the field?	☐	☐	☐	☐

Chapter 10 Audit—Sales

	Yes	No	Not Sure	N/A
1. Do I feel that new product launches are carefully planned and fully developed before products are introduced in the field?	☐	☐	☐	☐
2. Do I receive sales aids and tools in a timely enough manner so that I can understand and learn to use them correctly before going to the field?	☐	☐	☐	☐
3. Do I receive an adequate level of training on new products so that I feel comfortable when presenting them to prospects?	☐	☐	☐	☐
4. Do I feel that we introduce too many new products to the marketplace?	☐	☐	☐	☐
5. Do I feel that new products have gone through adequate and testing before being released?	☐	☐	☐	☐
6. Do I feel that I know enough about competitive products or services when I take new products to the field?	☐	☐	☐	☐
7. Does my organization actively solicit my feedback about the response that new products are receiving in the field?	☐	☐	☐	☐
8. Do I feel that the feedback I give is acted on in a timely and productive manner?	☐	☐	☐	☐
9. Do I receive updated training and sales tools on new products as needed?	☐	☐	☐	☐

Index